I0092867

USING MY WORD POWER

Advocating For A More Civilized Society

BOOK I: ETHICS AND VALUES

REAL ADVOCACY JOURNALISM® Series

JANICE S. ELLIS, PhD

USARiseUp, Inc.

Using My Word Power: Advocating for a More Civilized Society
Book I: Ethics and Values
Real Advocacy Journalism® Series

Copyright © 2022 by Janice S. Ellis, PhD

BISAC Codes: 1. POL046000; 2. POL043000; 3. SOC070000; 4. SOC028000; 5. SOC031000

All rights reserved. No part of this publication may be reproduced, distributed, or transmitted in any form or by any means, including photocopying, recording, scanning, or other electronic or mechanical methods without the prior written permission of the publisher or author. For permission requests, contact the publisher or author.

ISBN: 979-8-218-04479-4 (paperback)
ISBN: 979-8-218-04596-8 (hardcover)
ISBN: 979-8-218-04597-5 (digital)

Library of Congress Control Number: 2022943760

Cover design by Lewis Agrell

USARiseUp, Inc.
6320 Brookside Plaza, #275
Kansas City, MO 64213
844-931-2200

https://realadvocacyjournalism.com

Printed in the United States Of America

ALSO, BY JANICE S. ELLIS

From Liberty to Magnolia:
In Search of the American Dream (2018)

Shaping Public Opinion:
How *Real Advocacy Journalism*™ Should Be Practiced (2021)

Dedication

To those who believe that our words and actions matter
in advancing a more civilized and better society

To my parents, Stafford and Mable Holden Scott, who instilled a
strong foundation of ethics and values in me and my six siblings

Reviews

"*Using My Word Power: Advocating for a More Civilized Society* focuses on *Ethics and Values.* It is the first of a 3-book series, drawing important connections between words and actions as it discusses a myriad of contemporary issues ranging from gun usage to global warming, racism, and economics.

Lessons from the black experience in America and major thinkers about policy-setting and social issues come into play as Dr. Ellis considers a range of issues relating to national values and the changing course and nature of American politics and society.

The first thing to note about her work is that it comes from the perspective of an active journalist who not only reports on these conditions, but participates in the democratic process of enacting change.

This allows for a more personal and passionate tone that's injected into the mix of reflections, creating an accessible document of American experience that resonates on personal as well as political levels because of this background and focus: '*The writings of an advocate journalist always boil down, directly, or indirectly, intentionally, or unintentionally, to a plea—imploring the reader or listener to think, to consider the facts, the cir-*

cumstances, the workable solutions for the issues at hand, and when appropriate and necessary to engage in action.'

The book contains commentaries written over the past four decades for radio, a major metropolitan daily newspaper, community newspapers, an online state news publication, and the author's website. The commentaries have been chosen for their timeliness as well as timelessness. They also reflect snapshots of history.

The writings tackle a myriad of evolving situations and present candid analysis that often conclude in a plea for reconsideration on the reader's part: *'Given the circumstances, to wear a mask is the least that we as Americans can do for ourselves, our family, our neighbors, the overworked doctors and nurses, shuttered businesses, and the health and economic well-being of America. To wear a mask or not wear a mask? Please consider the consequences of your answer to that question.'*

These wide-ranging questions also emphasize the power of words to outline, convince, and provide alternate perspectives, making these pieces perfect for book clubs, debates, and other interactive forms of dialogue from high school into adult circles.

The result of these works is an effective example of how the written word can change hearts and minds through powerful writing and meaningful discourse.

Here are the keys to not just employing but reading and interpreting words wisely. Replete in examples of ethical and moral conundrums, *Using My Word Power* serves as the starting point for effecting change, and is highly recommended for a variety of libraries and book reading groups, from those that focus on contemporary social issues and questions of ethical and moral value to others who seek examples of powerful literacy's effects on society as a whole."

— D. Donovan, Senior Book Reviewer
Midwest Book Reviews

"A veteran writer offers guidance for future advocacy journalists in this first installment of a nonfiction trilogy.

Dedicated 'to those who believe that our words and actions matter in advancing a more civilized and better society,' this book is built on the principle that advocacy journalism is essential to a thriving democracy. With a doctorate in communication arts from the University of Wisconsin, Ellis has an expertise in the field that includes solid academic underpinnings and four decades of experience as an advocacy journalist whose commentary and writings have appeared on radio and blogs and in newspapers. Teaching by example, the book mostly reprints articles that provide readers not only with expert commentary on race relations from the perspective of a Black woman, but also models for neophyte writers. To Ellis, far too many of today's advocacy journalists are willing to sacrifice facts and fairness for partisan propaganda and sensationalism. Alternately, the author implores readers to see advocacy journalism as 'a plea' that entreats people 'to think, to consider the facts, the circumstances, the workable solutions for the issues at hand, and when appropriate and necessary to engage in action.' More than just offering wisdom for today's budding journalists, as a Black writer born in Mississippi who remembers 'the humiliation' of segregation firsthand, Ellis gives readers of all vocations a sage voice. She blends solid research with well-reasoned arguments on issues that range from interracial marriage and gun control to Confederate statues and Native American mascots. Divided into two parts ('Humanity Dignity Respect' and 'Commemorations'), the book offers concise articles and commentaries centered on the overarching theme of 'Ethics and Values,' delivering 'real' advocacy journalism. ... The author is a master journalist who skillfully balances her passionate takes with objective facts and effectively deploys 'the only real and lasting weapon' people have: their words.

A potent ode to the power of advocacy journalism."

— Kirkus Reviews
The most trusted voice in book reviews since 1933

"*Using My Word Power: Advocating for a More Civilized Society* is a compilation of essays by advocate journalist Janice S. Ellis that prompts the reader to ask: how can we make America a better, stronger nation?

These articles, ranging from as early as 1976 up until recent days, make it clear that disturbingly, in many matters, little has changed in the forty-some years since

Ellis's first piece was published. There continues to be gun violence, mass shootings, drug abuse both elicit and prescription, racial violence, and climate change denial. As one essay points out: climate change and racism have in common that some people refuse to believe either exists, despite overwhelming evidence. Each essay has its date revealed only at the end of it, showing that each work could be about the present day.

Using My Word Power is a First Place winner of the Nellie Bly Nonfiction Journalism Award.

Janice S. Ellis's work is thoughtful, enlightening and, moreover, timeless. Highly Recommended!"

— Chanticleer International Book Reviews

Contents

Part Two: Commemorations

Introduction

I have been an advocate journalist for the past four decades, which is nothing short of a miracle when you take into account that I was raised on a small cotton farm in Mississippi. Against all odds, as someone from a generation that can still vividly remember the humiliation of being forced to sit down at the back of the bus, I graduated from a highly respected university with a PhD.

My life experiences, during what has been a very turbulent period of history for the Black community in an ever-evolving America, have profoundly shaped my opinion pieces written for radio, several newspapers, and now online. I have loved and lost, given birth and reared children, weathered verbal, and physical abuse from trusted lovers, recovered from colossal failures—all while navigating American life, as a woman, Black, or as a Black and a woman, forever fighting against allowing either of those indelible birthmarks to define me, or confine me. More about the trials and triumphs of my life are described in my memoir, *From Liberty to Magnolia: In Search of the American Dream*.

As circumstances, issues, and forces—social, political, economic—occur all around me, push against me, I have chosen to push back. I have consciously entered and continue to enter the fray, using the power of words—the only real and lasting weapon I have.

Being a journalist has not been my formal training nor my profession. Becoming an advocate journalist has been my calling. I have always, since leaving graduate school and seeking to find my productive place in society, kept pen and paper—now a smartphone or notepad—near to capture an idea, a thought, or a plea, regarding some human condition, some public policy issue, or some social problem. I have even written complete commentary on cocktail napkins during a return flight from a business trip, after having put my briefcase or computer in the overhead bin. I dared not to have taken the chance to retrieve either and run the risk of losing the idea, the message, more akin to a plea, which beckoned to be expressed.

The writings of an advocate journalist always boil down, directly, or indirectly, intentionally, or unintentionally, to a plea—imploring the reader or listener to think, to consider the facts, the circumstances, the workable solutions for the issues at hand, and when appropriate and necessary to engage in action.

As a woman, a black, a wife, a mother, a career professional, and carrying out my calling to be an advocate journalist, I have primarily addressed some of the enduring issues of our times. But also, I could not ignore the temporal—pressing issues of the hour. Most of my writings during the last four decades have maintained their relevancy, fulfilling a needed voice albeit often crying in a wilderness or falling on deft ears and blind eyes.

As a collection, my commentaries are snapshots of history. One of my newspaper editors characterizes my commentaries as "evergreens." For that I am grateful. That characterization has kept me writing when in those infrequent moments I have asked, "Why am I bothering to write anything?"

During the past four decades, the commentaries have been written for a large radio station, a major metropolitan daily newspaper, community newspapers, as a guest columnist for a metropolitan business journal, and currently online.

Regardless of the medium of communication, I have tried to adhere to the standards of what I call *Real Advocacy Journalism*™, which is covered in detail in my award-winning book, *Shaping Public Opinion: How Real Advocacy*™ *Should Be Practiced*, (2021).

What is the difference between advocacy journalism as it is practiced today and *Real Advocacy Journalism*® that is described and advanced in the book?

Much of the advocacy journalism practiced today is partisan, biased, and often blurs the lines between truth and lies, facts and fiction, and often presents fake news as real news. The purpose and objectives of such advocacy journalism constitute propaganda to gain public support for the interest and agenda of a few, a special interest group, or a small constituency rather than for the good of the majority.

Advocacy journalism across different media has become a pernicious tool often carried out by partisans, zealots, and extremists, pushing separatist ideologies rather than unity, without any mention or consideration for objectivity or transparency. This is evident in print media with publications focused solely on targeted agendas such as conservative, liberal, the far right, the far left. It is also evident in electronic media with cable stations and programs whose content is designed to present and support only one side of the issue or political spectrum, covering only one type of incidents or stories that occur rather than presenting all sides, and covering all aspects as accurately as possible. There is often little or no effort to present the complete picture.

These practices have given rise to the idea, the notion, even concern about whether there is systemic media bias that pervades contemporary public communication and discourse.

Complex local, regional, national, and global issues are often covered and treated with a biased and simplistic categorization. This happens all too frequently when the public is asked to form an opinion or support an action. Historically, and currently, this occurs in issue areas such as: should we go to war or support a war; what is the appropriate health care policy for the majority of citizens; how can gun violence be curbed; what are the distinctions between terrorism carried out by a foreign enemy, naturalized citizen, or a naturally born citizen; is climate change a real threat to civilization or a man-made hoax; is the Covid-19 pandemic a massive conspiracy; and, on and on....

A constant barrage of simplistic, distorted, biased, untruthful, non-factual treatments can only be a disservice to a dependent, hopeful, ill-informed, trusting public.

What passes as legitimate advocacy journalism is often characterized by rumors, inuendo, conspiracy theories, sensationalism, and all kinds of drama that is carried out in mainstream media, social media, and most critically in conversations, presentations, and public forums—within whatever orbit of influence of the practitioner—all reinforcing false information that leads to further divisiveness, poor policy decisions, detrimental actions, and sometimes apathy with no actions at all when they are critically needed. Evidence of this is addressed in detail in *Shaping Public Opinion*.

In my writings, I have endeavored to stick to the facts, analyze them, put an event, situation, or issues into perspective in order to foster a better understanding, and provide direction to form an opinion or pursue an action. We all live and function in an orbit of influence. How in-depth a particular commentary addresses a subject matter has been determined by the time allotted for the radio spot, the space in a newspaper, or word count online.

I do not proclaim that each and every one of my commentaries have been exhaustive on a particular subject or met all the noble standards of *Real Advocacy Journalism*®. But adhering to those standards in providing a meaningful perspective has always been my goal.

In surveying my writings over the past four decades—from 1976 through 2021—their focus can be organized in three categories: Ethics and Values; Justice and Equality; and Patriotism and Politics, and I have compiled them in three books accordingly.

This is Book I, Ethics and Values, of three books in the *Real Advocacy Journalism*® series. Book II focuses on Justice and Equality. Book III addresses Patriotism and Politics.

In each book, the commentaries have been grouped under major section headings. As a prelude in each section, I have selected one of the first commentaries written and delivered in a 2-minute spot on WISN radio, the largest ABC affiliate, located in Milwaukee, Wisconsin. All commentaries, written across the decades, have been chosen for their enduring relevancy in terms of the **timeliness**, or **timelessness** of their subject matter—then and now. Many represent historical accounts of defining moments, incidents, and issues that have had lasting impact and lessons learned.

Following the initial two years of delivering commentaries on WISN radio, columns were written for newspapers over three decades. During the last ten years, they have appeared online. All commentaries published online at JaniceSEllis.com and The Missouri Independent contain evidentiary links that are inaccessible in the printed version but can be accessed on the respective websites. The dates and where the commentaries appeared/appear are found at the end of each.

My hope is that in sharing my attempts to improve understanding about issues that impact us all that you will be informed, enlightened, inspired and have reaffirmation that in addition to our beliefs, our words and actions are what advances a more civilized and better society.

Part One

Humanity Dignity Respect

Our core values and sense of ethics are manifested in how we regard all of humanity, how we exhibit and express dignity and respect in our conduct toward ourselves, others, and the communities of which we are apart. That is the focus of this collection of commentaries.

Prelude: Knowing Oneself Is the Key

We have all heard, at one time or another, phrases inspired and written by the great Socrates and Plato, like "know thyself," or, Shakespeare's "to thine own self be true," from *Hamlet*, and the line, "If you can keep your head when all about you are losing theirs..." from the famous poem "If" by Rudyard Kipling.

Well, call them what you will: great quotes from philosophy and literature, mere platitudes, or just commonsense phrases. However, they are regarded, if we would pause to give them serious thought and reflection from time to time, we would find that they are loaded with important meaning.

Examine the first phrase, "know thyself." How many of us really do? Coming to know oneself requires deep, frequent, and candid self-examination. If we take the time to examine ourselves, we might realize the benefits are well worth the time and the probing. For example, one can arrive at a realistic view of skills, talents, and areas of interest and passion. This accurate assessment helps a person decide what career to pursue or which careers to avoid. Many people spend a lifetime doing jobs they do not enjoy and half-heartedly perform the tasks the job requires.

A person may have some accurate measure of what their abilities are and what allows them to withstand the natural and contrived problems that may otherwise deter or even defeat them.

Knowing oneself also means realizing that a person has an identity—certain characteristics that set them apart from anyone else. Discovery of this identity will prevent them from jumping on the bandwagon or falling prey to any social fad that comes along.

But to know oneself is a continual process. Various experiences in life bring about changes within us. We must be ever aware of these changes—understanding how they occurred and why.

Getting to know oneself is much like getting to know another person. We have to keep an open mind and an open eye, making adjustments in what we think and see as we go along. Once we know ourselves, then we can better understand, appreciate, and apply other phrases like "to thine own self be true." And indeed, we will be able to "keep our heads when those all about [us] are losing theirs." Or, if we do not, we will at least know and understand why.

Delivered on June 27, 1976
WISN Radio, Milwaukee, Wisconsin

Living in Denial Personally or Professionally

No matter our circumstances, conditions, or opportunities, living in denial personally or professionally will always undermine the potential of achieving the best outcomes for all involved. While denying that something negative has occurred or exists might provide comfort, that comfort is only illusive and temporary.

Our daily lives are replete with examples of where we allow denial to creep in, even rule what we say and do. We see it in our families, our communities, in our state, in our nation. At the family level, there may be a member suffering from mental illness or substance abuse, but we refuse to accept or believe it. We rationalize that it is temporary, a phase, rather than confronting it the instance we suspect it or after we have seen mounting evidence. Who benefits in such a circumstance? Not the person, nor the family. Living in denial personally or professionally benefits no one.

In our communities, we may witness youths wandering aimlessly, with no meaningful educational support or recreational activities to improve the chances of them becoming young adults leading productive fulfilled lives. As parents, caring adults, and professionals across the vocational spectrum, aren't we living in denial personally and professionally when we chose to turn a blind eye yet expect these youths not to fall in harm's way or resort to a life of delinquency and crime?

At the state and national level when we witness elected officials, time and time again, acting, speaking, and supporting policies that are contrary to the best interest of the people, the state, or the country, what are we to think? What are we to do when we witness not only the steady lack of progress, but the decline in many areas of our collective lives? Increasing gun violence. Unequal access to health care. Unfair taxation. Race and gender inequality. Climate change. Internal and external threats to our democracy. Living in denial personally and professionally will not help up confront these real challenges. Denial will only delay, even prevent, us from arriving at workable solutions.

There is freedom, there is empowerment, even peace and motivation when we are willing individually and collectively to stop living in denial personally and professionally and begin to deal forthrightly with what is going on in our private and public lives. There is much to be gained in improving conditions and circumstances all around. That is the only way real progress, real solutions can be achieved.

As painful or as fearful as it might be, we all must stop living in denial personally and professionally. Not to do so will result in the ultimate denial of all—forfeiting and never achieving the best lives that we can have—all around.

Published June 6, 2021
https://janicesellis.com/blog

A Beautiful Picture Can Often Hide a Multitude of Faults

Too often, we define the state of our health and happiness, our security and prosperity by the state of our pocketbook or bank accounts. If we are able to afford and enjoy the kind of lifestyle that we desire—whether that is defined by a type of house, a kind of automobile, how many times we go out for dinner, go out on the town, or simply how much money we may have squirreled away—we somehow equate those things with a state of well-being.

On a more global scale, we seem to think that when we have a strong economy, low unemployment rates, and good consumer buying, then things generally are in great shape, and all is well whether we are talking about our city, state, or nation.

But is all really well?

And are these material and tangible indicators an accurate measure? Can we really gauge the well-being of a neighborhood, city, or country by how well it looks or how it seems to be prospering? What may appear to be good and great often hide a myriad of problems.

Let us take a closer look at the bigger picture for the makeup and contents of the canvas only reflect and mirror what is happening on a smaller scale. Some would and could argue that it is the other way around. But at any rate, whether you choose to examine the big picture or just a small snapshot of what is being painted as the state of our wellbeing, you might find some disturbing conditions—cracks in the dam.

Let's look at one scene from the big picture. America has enjoyed unprecedented and sustained economic growth for the last ten years. Unemployment is at an all-time low. Inflation hardly exists. We are considered the strongest and wealthiest nation on earth in many categories.

But did you know we are also considered one of the most violent nations? You might ask how this can be when you can hardly turn on the evening news and not here reports of casualties in some civil war some place in the world.

But we as Americans experience more handgun violence than any other place on the planet. Just think about it. This year alone, gun violence penetrated nearly every walk of our lives. We commonly think of gun violence when a drug deal goes bad in the streets, or a robbery is foiled. We also know that deaths by handguns happen far too often in the home whether intentional or accidental. But this year, deaths and injuries have occurred in schools, the workplace, day care centers, even the church—by a person or persons hell bent on killing somebody, any-body.

And we think all is well during these times of growth and prosperity. Well, think again.

As we experience prosperity and plenty, we have had more violence toward children, sometimes committed by children, and too often at the hands of sick uncaring adults.

While we may feel we have made more gains in race relations and tolerance of those who may be different, we have had more hate crimes than we care to think about.

At a time of educational and technological advance-ment, we have more children failing to make the grade and moving toward a lifestyle and future that will not even approach those of their parents, yet along exceed it.

We used to think of terrorist acts as occurring beyond our shores. That we as American were insulated from such vicious and cowardly deeds, but during this decade we have been shaken from that false sense of security. And each of us probably has some trepidation as we approach the new millennium, as authorities anticipate and pre-pare for the possibility of some terrorist act right her on our soil.

And we think all is well during these times of growth and prosperity. Well, we need to think again.

We must see how we can take a section of the canvass and do whatever we can to make sure it reflects the real picture. We must scratch beneath the surface and do what we can to diffuse ticking time bombs. Do what we can to mend and repair broken spirits. Do what we can to help realize dreams. This also means that the painting is never finished.

The real lasting health and wellbeing of our neighborhoods, our city, our state, our nation depends on it.

Published January 4, 2010
USAonRace.com

Closing The Intergenerational Divide:
Golden Years Can Be a Gold Mine

We have become a culture that overlooks one of our most valuable, and available, resources—our senior citizens.

The month of May has been designated as "Older Americans Month." Events are planned to celebrate aging by sharing information on how to optimize health and lead active, more productive lives.

I have always had mixed feeling about the need to designate a month for this or that. It usually signals an area or issue that we are neglectful of or oblivious about in our everyday lives. We have just completed two such designations: February as Black History month, and April as Child Abuse Prevention month.

There are other designations, whether days, weeks, or months, dispersed across the calendar, pleading for our collective attention. Such neglect of people, places, or things, intentional or benign, usually means there is a cost associated with it. Sometimes monetarily, sometimes, and more importantly, in the toll it takes on humanity.

We have paid, and continue to pay, dearly on both aspects of the cost equation when we examine how this society regards and treats it aging citizens.

Whether you are considered a part of generation X, Y, or a baby boomer, it is just a matter of time that we join the senior citizen band. So, from where does this short-sightedness come?

Just think about it. It begins at about age thirty. There is a mindset that the biological clock, along with the career clock, begins to wind down or races at an accelerated rate. We become consumed, if not obsessed, by the nagging thought that we have only a few years to parade our plumes, strut our stuff, procreate, and land that plum corporate position that will allow us to drive our dream car, live in our dream house in our dream neighborhood.

This perception is reinforced by the advertising industry, which often promotes youthfulness often at the expense of aging.

What a waste for all involved. Senior citizens are, and will continue to be, a gold mine of useful resources for those who are often trying to find their way on roads already traveled. One only has to look at current and future population trends to see what great resources seniors will continue to be.

According to the 2000 Census, thirty-five million Americans, about 13 percent, are sixty-five years and over. This is a ten-fold increase since 1900. This number will show a significant increase in the 2010 Census as the nation's baby boomers enter their golden years. Over the next 30 years, the elderly population is projected to double.

Just as America is a community of all races, we can easily add that it is also a community of all ages. Such an emphasis pays tribute to the strength of communities that is a result of the richness that multi-generational families bring.

Shouldn't we be about developing more opportunities where we can have meaningful and enriching interactions across generations, where older adults are working with children and youth to enrich each other's lives? Older Americans can be enlisted to do much more than staff polling sites during elections, and volunteer for the various domestic and foreign aid organizations.

While such volunteer efforts are worthy and laudable endeavors, much of what seniors have to offer is unappreciated and underutilized.

Perhaps a lasting value to be gained from this year's month-long celebration is to think of ways older members of our families, neighborhoods, social and professional clubs can become engaged in meaningful ways with the children and youth around them. Many are in desperate need of the wisdom, experience, and nurturing that older generations can readily bring.

There are programs that seek to provide just that. The Foster Grandparent program most readily comes to mind. No doubt many retired teachers and other professionals volunteer as tutors and mentors at neighborhood schools and in their churches.

When we look at the state of well-being of our children and youth across America whether it is performance in schools or the rate of alcohol and substance abuse, we know that much more pairing needs to be done.

And it is not just a one-way street. What opportunities exist for young people to serve the elderly, who may be frail, confined to home or in some other assisted living environment. Imagine the mutually beneficial and enjoyable experience of a first or second grader reading a half-hour a week to a senior citizen, or a seventh grader getting a better sense of history from someone who lived through the Depression or World War II.

Many problems that plague contemporary society do not require more money, but rather the realization that the solution could lie with those who have been there and done that.

Only if we all—baby boomers, generations X, Y and Z—would pause in our worship and obsession with youthfulness long enough to see.

Published May 3, 2010
USAonRace.com

What Is Happening to Our Quest to Become a More Civilized Society?

Will you become a pistol-packing mamma or a gun-toting dude? What will be your piece of choice? A pearl-handled derringer? A 44 magnum? Or, will you take no chances and carry a fifteen-round semi-automatic berretta in your briefcase?

Soon, if it is left up to many states and their respective legislators (with Arizona ahead of most), you will have that choice. We all may have a chance, firsthand, to experience many aspects of the good old days of the "Wild, Wild West" all across America. Whether we like it or not, at any point, we could be in the midst of a shootout at the Okay Car Wash or witness a real live duel at the Dairy Queen.

Imagine getting into a little verbal skirmish in the parking lot, and your irate assailant reaching in a pocket, purse or glove compartment and you are not sure if they will pull out a slip of gum or a loaded gun. Imagine some possible outcomes of road rage. The specter of being hit by a speeding bullet will put dodging potholes in a whole different perspective.

Not to mention the increased number of children who will arrive in the emergency rooms of area hospitals either injured, barely hanging on to life, marred for life, or maybe with no life left in them at all. All because they, in their innocence and ignorance, picked up a gun carelessly left in a pocket, a purse, underneath a car seat and discharged it—hurting or killing themselves or others.

Aren't there enough accidental deaths and acts of gun violence perpetrated by adults and children alike? What is there to be gained by making it easier to have more guns in public places? One of the most common arguments is that it will help deter crime and improve self-protection.

But will more guns reduce crime and enhance our ability to protect ourselves? What is the likelihood that if you are surprised by a burglar or accosted that you would actually have the opportunity to pull your gun, get the upper hand on the assailant and shoot him or her first? Imagine walking down the streets or in the park. Will strangers—even the criminally suspicious ones—likely smile, nod and keep strolling because our mutual epiphany is, "We both are probably carrying."

These are not the movies.

Fundamentally, one must ask whether "Conceal and Carry" is more of a gun control issue or a public safety issue. Will the proliferation of guns improve the

safety of those in our society who need the most protection—our children, the elderly? Will giving mostly
everyone the right to carry a concealed gun anywhere
and everywhere make our schools, neighborhoods,
parks, streets, shopping mall, churches, hospitals safer?

Many previous attempts to pass legislation allowing citizens to carry concealed guns, failed. But, today,
more and more we seem to be more accepting. Such
legislation exists in many states.

To what do we attribute this growing interest in allowing
guns to be carried in public places? 9/11? Increasing specu-
lation as well as evidence that there are potential terrorists
among us wishing to do us harm? The proliferation of illegal
guns in the hands of criminals despite the gun control laws
already on the books? Is it a growing feeling that if we are
armed, then we can protect ourselves from some crime or
act of violence better than law enforcement officers?

When you think of the many innocent people who
fall victim to those who carry guns legally and illegally,
where does the answer lie?

America already has long held the unenviable position and reputation of being the most violent industrialized country on the planet. Why on earth do we think
that if most of us begin carrying guns that we have a
chance of changing the tide and trend of violence?

Why do we believe that an encounter between a
law-abiding and a law-breaking citizen, both carrying
guns, will yield a better outcome?

Carrying guns is the answer to achieving a more civilized society? What does this portend for civilization and our planet?

Published April 3, 2011
USAonRace.com

Guns, Crimes, and Police Brutality

Guns, crimes, and incidents of police brutality, what do they have in common? They seem to be as much a part of American culture as apple pie. What does that say about one of the most civilized, compassionate, and wealthiest nation on earth?

Some things that are not very flattering in the least, and hugely shameful and in so many ways un-American at worst. For this is not the image of America that any of us who loves this country should want, and as the America that many other countries look to as a world leader.

How can a world leader be content to be among the most violent nations in the world, has the highest rate of gun violence, and the most human beings locked up behind bars? How do we continue to tolerate and accept racial, educational, economic inequality and injustices of any kind that have gotten us to this point?

What does that say about our value set and our tolerance to continue to let such trends be acceptable to our way of life? Guns, crimes, and police brutality, what do they have in common in America?

There are more than three hundred million guns, legally and illegally, in circulation on the streets, in households, business establishments, and with the passage of some recent state laws, now in the legislative branches of government.

Essentially, there are enough guns out there that nearly every man, woman, and child could have one. And yet, gun laws are being relaxed or unenforced to make guns even more accessible.

Crime has almost become an expected way of life, especially in the core of most major cities where high unemployment among Blacks and other minorities seems immutable even when the national unemployment rate has move to 5.4%, lower than in has been in almost a decade. Yet unemployment in inner cities among minorities remains stubbornly in the double digits in many places.

Persistent unemployment is compounded by poor housing, blighted neighborhoods, sub-standard schools, and a pernicious sense of hopelessness when it comes to believing that there are realistic options to make things better or to ever escape. So entire communities become a breeding ground for crime.

Crime often involves guns, whether it is assault, burglary, drug trafficking and use, murder, or petty theft.

It is little wonder that aggressive policing and incidents of police brutality have become more prevalent in communities across America, particularly in the poorest, high crime and gun infested ones that are primarily black and have become ticking time bombs, where on any given day an otherwise common occurrence can ignite a major explosion.

Guns, crime, and incidents of police brutality will continue to be a large part of America's image, and way of life, until we commit to doing the things to bring about real change. The actions needed vary by community. But we all know what some of them are. Admit it.

There are many countries, less wealthy than America, where high crime rates, rampant gun violence and growing incidences of police brutality are not a major part of their landscape.

What does that say about us, America? When will we finally address these damning issues?

Published May 12, 2015
https://janicesellis.com/blog

America Has Millions More Guns Than People

There is something drastically wrong when America has millions more guns than people in homes, in communities, and in the streets. One can hardly turn to the local news without hearing, almost daily, someone being injured or killed in their home, car, or in the street—both intentional and accidental. This has nothing to do with 2nd Amendment rights.

Turn to the national news and it is becoming more common to hear of mass killings in homes, schools, churches, grocery stores, shopping malls, and other places where unsuspecting people have gathered, carrying out routine activities in their daily lives. And yet, those in power who can do something about it seem not to care that America has millions more guns that people.

The United States has more guns circulating all around us than any other civilized country in the world. Each year, America has more people to die by gun violence than in other advanced country. Have you ever thought about how uncivilized we are when it comes to solving conflicts? Don't you find it disturbing that America has millions more guns than people? Are you the least bit concern that almost 400 million guns of all kinds—legally—are among us? There is also an unknown number of illegal guns.

We want to boast of being the most humane and advanced democracy in the world. Yet, we are comfortable keeping, allowing, and using guns as viable alternatives to solve our conflicts, disagreements, and fears, rather than words, the rule of law, and value for human life. It cannot be said enough, every sensible adult should be very concerned that America has millions more guns than people.

Guns continue to proliferate and are available to and accessible by almost anyone. While there are laws about who can legally own guns, and laws requiring background checks and gun registrations, there are many loopholes and failures of enforcement. Many mass shootings by sane, deranged, distraught, or terrorist individuals occurred as a result of them being able to purchase guns legally. The gun problem is further exacerbated by the fact that no one has a handle on all the guns in circulation illegally. America has millions more guns than people, and the malady seems to be growing.

Does that seem like we are advancing as a civilized society? Have you ever thought about the state of affairs, if the proliferation of guns and indiscriminate killings continue? No one is immune to being the victim of gun violence—not children, not innocent bystanders, not the elderly, the disabled, not those trying to enforce the law and keep the peace—not anyone.

America has millions more guns than people, hidden and in plain view. Does it matter? Are you concerned for your family, your children, your community, your city, your nation?

Published May 16, 2021
https://janicesellis.com/blog

Monitoring System for Law Enforcement Agencies

Should the US Department of Justice establish a monitoring system for law enforcement agencies to ensure public safety similar to what the Federal Aviation Administration (FAA) has to monitor the airline industry?

The FAA has many rules, regulations, and oversight processes in place to ensure that citizens can fly safely. Those oversight processes and monitoring procedures do not just cover the physical quality and conditions of airplanes, or just ensuring that the air traffic control systems and controllers are doing their jobs accurately. The FAA has policies and procedures in place for issuing, suspending, or revoking pilot certificates, which the airline carriers must adhere to. Why can't there be a similar monitoring system for law enforcement agencies across the country?

We can hardly turn on the news without learning of a police officer or several police officers using excessive and deadly force, particularly when it comes to arresting black men. This is not just occurring in police departments in certain areas of the country. It seems to be happening in cities and towns coast to coast, in the north, south, east, and west. This random, wanton, and frequent inhumane conduct should be evidence enough that a monitoring system for law enforcement agencies needs to be put in place at the US Department of Justice that would apply to all police departments and officers.

Currently, the Department of Justice gets involved when a complaint of Civil Rights violations has been filed or when the public account of police brutality is so egregious that the department initiates an investigation on its own. Taking actions after the fact is clearly not enough because the incidents of brutality and excessive force keep repeating themselves. A monitoring system for law enforcement agencies need to be put in place to minimize, if not prevent, bad and illegal conduct on the part of police just as there are those that deal with the conduct and behavior of pilots.

The safety of citizens and the public must be enforced and monitored in police departments all across the country. This does not mean that there will be less support for police, or putting a stop to certain inhuman and deadly practices is punitive or restrictive when it comes to an officer doing his or her job. Everyone in every profession must adhere to rules of conduct. A monitoring system for law enforcement agencies could help ensure proper police conduct across the board.

If the priority of police departments all across the country is the safety of ALL citizens—white, black, brown, or yellow—who live in the communities, towns, and cities they serve, then they should not have any objections to having their policies and practices monitored. They, in fact, should be proud and proactive about displaying and reporting their stellar conduct of public safety. They, of all people, should have nothing to hide.

Where is the monitoring system for law enforcement agencies? Having one in place at the US Department of Justice is long past due.

Published May 23, 2021
https://janicesellis.com/blog

More Debtors Going to Prison: The Rise of Oppressive Capitalism in America

How prevalent is the practice of putting American citizens in jail for not being able to pay their debt? It is a practice, the prevalence of which is worth examining especially in these economically challenging times. Not to so is to allow a practice found in a more uncivilized society to tarnish how the American ideal of capitalism and individual rights should work together for the common good.

About six months ago, the *Wall Street Journal (WSJ)* reported that in more than a third of the states that borrowers who are unable or simply do not pay their debts can be sent to jail. It is one thing for those who are able to be sent to jail for not paying their debts, it is quite another to send someone to jail if they have lost their job, who are not working at all or for substantially-less wages.

The national statistics show that the practice of jailing debtors has increased since the onset of the financial crisis during the last several years. Many states are allowing this even though the Supreme Court ruled back in 1983 that such practice is illegal and a violation of an American citizen's Fourteenth Amendment Rights. It appears that aggressive collection agencies are finding loopholes to drag often the unsuspecting, unemployed, or underemployed into court—an appearance that sometimes results in the debtor going to jail.

According to another report in the *WSJ*, while some states are trying to stop the practice of borrowers actually being put in jail, the threat of arrest continues to surge.

How is it that this increasing trend is not getting more attention in the political debates on the economy this election year, by any candidates for elective office—either at the local, state, or national level? Is it a matter of the burden of the little guy once again getting ignored or subjugated to the benefit of the "system" or powerful capitalist?

Who would you guess is most frequently dragged into court for being unable to pay a debt? Yes, the unemployed, the working poor, most of whom are minorities, already downtrodden, and carrying a disproportionate burden in trying to realize some elements of the American dream.

It also begs the question what is the point of jailing the debtor. How will that improve the prospect of the creditor getting repaid? Furthermore, what sense does it make for creditors to condone or allow the vigilante tactics of unscrupulous collection agencies? Are these the tactics we are resorting to, or turning a blind eye, to make free enterprise work?

Fortunately, there are some states that are requiring that collection agencies prove that debtors have willfully not paid and ignored written notifications that they are being sued for a debt or are required to appear in court. The Federal Trade Commission has also begun to take legal actions of their own, taking seriously some of the hundreds of thousands of complaints received annually against collection agencies, and filing suits of their own.

But, isn't putting poor, under or unemployed people in jail a moral and ethical question worthy of attention in the political debates on the state of the nation's economy? Frankly, isn't it un-American not to do so?

Where is the plight of the poor and downtrodden on the list of priorities for any candidate vying to lead—at the national, state, or local level? Whose interests are they serving?

While some borrowers may be guilty of being slick or derelict when it comes to honoring their commitment to pay their debts, most struggling Americans are hardworking and honest, doing all they can during this protracted economic downturn.

Elected officials, and those aspiring to become leaders, need to take a stand on this one.

Published May 28, 2012
USAonRace.com

The Devastation of Drug Use: Can the Destructive Course Be Contained?

Drugs. The lure of drugs comes as a thief in the night, robbing us of our best and often our most promising. We are reminded as we mourn the death of Whitney Houston.

While the toxicology report is yet to be finalized, from the accounts of what transpired during the days prior to her death, and her long-term battle with substance abuse, it appears that alcohol and drugs had something to do with Houston's untimely death.

Drugs can be compared to the most forceful tornado, capable of destroying everything in its path: individual lives, families, homes, bank accounts, and too often innocent bystanders. The enticement to use has no respect of race, age, neighborhood, or profession. Through users and pushers, the indulgence is pervasive, becoming a social epidemic and private hell for too many of the vulnerable and unsuspecting.

Yes, we have known the presence and power of illegal drugs, whether it is heroin, cocaine, crack cocaine, methamphetamine, ecstasy, and other less pervasive substances. But legal prescription drugs are posing perhaps an even greater threat. A greater threat because their danger hides behind the trust and confidence of a physician or pharmacist who is willing to compromise the Hippocratic Oath for greed and glory. We have to ask, is this what the war on drugs has come to? A fight against illegal and legal drug dealers.

With the deaths of Michael Jackson, and now Whitney Houston, we are learning that boutique doctors and pharmacists are readily available to the rich and famous to provide them their drug of choice even when they know they can be deadly. The untimely deaths of Amy Winehouse and Keith Ledger are other instances.

Perhaps, Houston's death will be yet another wakeup call. But at what point, will we realize that a combination of alcohol and prescription drugs may be posing an even greater threat to ordinary people, member of our families, our children, our neighbors, or their children?

Losing someone like Whitney Houston is only symptomatic of larger societal woes. Does it really matter whether its cocaine, heroin, Xanax, or OxyContin? Drugs, the almighty tempests—they all shatter dreams, destroy beliefs, make the strong weak. We watch our heroes, friends and family members alike succumb to them.

The toll drugs are taking on every aspect of our society is staggering, is eating away at the very fabric of our society. And the long-term impact will be cataclysmic and far-reaching if we do not find the means to minimize and tear away the stranglehold.

There are many attempts at a local and national level to stop the proliferation and use of drugs. But we have to ask ourselves is anything working? There must be a concerted efforts by many—parents, churches, schools, and other agencies.

While we cannot give up on the adults who have fallen victim, our greatest effort must be directed toward our children. Our children are the most unsuspecting, the most vulnerable—those who cannot imagine the impact, the devastation on their lives should they elect to experiment with a drug that some uncaring, low-life pusher convinces them to try.

We must spend the time at every opportunity to show them the consequences of bad choices. It is incumbent upon every caring adult to warn them of the increasing dangers of drugs, and the potential prices people pay when they allow themselves to succumb to the thrills, the highs of the moment. It has to be our priority to help them to distinguish between fleeting moments of false happiness and false security and those of lasting fulfillment and true happiness.

How do we do this? Invest the time to teach our children about the value of thinking or using reasoning when confronted with tough choices. Life is filled with choices. We make them daily. But it only takes one wrong choice to shape the rest of one's life.

All of our children, black, white, brown, and yellow deserve our vigilance and intervention.

It will take the village to stand and say to drugs, "No, not ours."

Published June 21, 2012
USAonRace.com

Global Warming and Racism Likeness

What does global warming and racism have in common? Denial by many that either exists, despite seeing signs and examples all around us.

Racism, like global warming, is pervasive and destructive. Their negative impact is preventable, but only if we are willing to open our minds and believe that they exist. Only then will we care enough to put forth any concerted and sustained effort to do something about either of them.

Many of us would like to believe that interracial issues, like global warming, pose no major problem in this country or in other parts of the world. But if we honestly looked around us, we would witness incidents almost on a daily basis that whisper or scream to us that bigotry like violent storms, prejudice like oppressive heat waves, and other signs of racism and global warming are part of our daily lives and the environment in which we live.

Both racism and global warming are occurring worldwide. Reports of incidents of racism or signs of climate change occur in United States, England, Ireland, South Africa, Zimbabwe, Canada, Israel, Greece, and other places near and far—from racial slurs and unexpected microbursts to racial violence and F6 tornados in the least expected places.

We are seeing it all unfold. At what point, will the importance of racism rise to the same level as the global issues that we must deal with such as the economy, terrorism, energy, education, and global warming? When will we spend the time and resources to get at these critical issues that in many ways undermine our ability to find meaningful and lasting solutions?

How do we effectively address what plagues our economy, our educational system, the fight against terrorism, solutions to global warming and the emerging energy crisis if we do not take time to better understand our differences, take time to celebrate what we hold in common and what binds us as human beings?

Silence, denial, and fear are the real enemy in tackling tough issues like global warming and racism.

Like the many changes occurring in our environment, we must take the time to understand the people of different colors and cultures if we ever plan to solve some of the daunting problems we face on planet earth and enrich our own lives in the process.

Published December 8, 2019
https://janicesellis.com/blog

Greed of the Most Grievous Kind

We have all witnessed or experienced the ravages of greed on some level, at some point in our lives.

Greed manifests itself in acceptable and repulsive ways. Acceptable: When merchants practice price gouging on their occasional and regular customers on an infrequent and frequents basis. When parents work to accumulate material things and future financial security at the expense of the emotional and developmental wellbeing of family members.

Repulsive: When drug dealers sell destructive substances to innocent unsuspecting children, and pimps pray on underage girls and entice them into the dark and demeaning world of prostitution. When professional thieves and ordinary thieves take advantage, pilfer, and financially rape the elderly.

That dual face of greed—these examples are only a few.

And then, there is Robert Courtney, the Kansas City pharmacist who by his own admission, according to Court records, diluted drugs administered to cancer patients. While his innocence or guilt remains to be determined, these alleged actions may have contributed to robbing those who were fighting to hang on and experience whatever vestiges of life they could as they fought some of the most evasive and pernicious cancers known to medical science.

While we have not had the trial or heard the case of what motivated Courtney to perpetrate these alleged acts of the most grievous kind on a cohort of his most vulnerable and dependent patients, according to Court records, Courtney said that greed was the driving force. Courtney's greed could have cheated and undermined, unknowingly to those affected, the gallant fight they are waging for life—all, apparently, to add to his financial coffers.

The results of his alleged actions on those directly affected, their families, the health care delivery system, and that frayed, and perhaps fleeting, domain called "public trust" are bound to be felt for a very long time.

A few poignant effects come to mind. The tremendous compromise of the affected patients' physical and mental well-being defies description. The magnitude and sense of betrayal felt by these patients and their loved ones is evidenced by the hundreds of calls received by the FBI hot line, and cases filed against Courtney. To say the ordeal has been numbing and simultaneously enraging is grossly understated.

It must leave the rest of us wondering what we are to make of the systems that we trust and rely upon to protect us. For example, investigators are still trying to sort out whether the pharmaceutical manufacturer responded appropriately in the public's best interest after the pharmaceutical sales representative raised a red flag of suspicion. If the manufacturer did not, why not? Was it to avoid the risk of a negative impact on their bottom line?

Given these egregious allegations, if proven to be true, can the average consumer believe and have faith that adequate regulations and controls are in place and this instance represents a rare exception? Really, how can we know?

What about those who will seize this opportunity to further exploit the systems, trying to extract any remuneration they can, justifiably or not? Should frivolous lawsuits emerge, who ultimately will pay? The vulnerable public, who is at the mercy of the system whether it is the medical community, the governmental regulatory agencies or law enforcement.

What ravenous violations one man's greed may have wrought.

There have been many writers, philosophers and prophets through the ages that have warned us about the power and perverseness of money. Perhaps one of the most renowned warnings comes from the New Testament writings of the apostle, Timothy when he pronounces: "The love of money is the root of all evil."

Money within itself is not evil, just the love of it.

The problems often come with the choices and actions taken in the quest to accumulate it.

There is still honor associated with money earned from a hard day's work, rather than at the expense of society's most vulnerable.

Robert Courtney's alleged actions are an incredibly sad reminder of when the uglier side of greed takes over and no matter how much honest money is earned, it seems not be enough.

It forces one to look deeper and be watchful of that threshold when the greed becomes the driving destructive force in a small or a major way.

The impact is still negative.

Published August 31, 2001
The Kansas City Star

When Money or Greed Means More than People

Unnecessary loss of life, injury, damage to one's health are just a few catastrophic and irreparable things that occur when money or greed means more than people in a capitalistic society. Is there any such thing as enough is enough? What will it take for perpetrators to be held accountable? There are related questions to be asked of governmental regulatory agencies, and us as a society.

These are all questions that come to mind as we watch the horrific collapse of a condominium in Surfside, Florida where it is feared that over 160 unsuspecting residents may have lost their lives in an instant. What a devastating, heartbreaking, and unavoidable tragedy. It has been revealed that a report warning of the structural deterioration of the building was issued more than 3 years ago. Why weren't steps taken immediately, by building owners and everyone who was aware, to fix it? When money or greed means more than people, it is always a matter of time before a calamity occurs.

While we do not want to be unduly alarmed, it begs the questions what other disasters could be looming. What is even worse is how many warnings and reports have been filed to make companies and governmental agencies aware of dangerous conditions that need to be corrected to no avail. Recalls are fairly common in the automobile, food, and toy industries. But how many such reports and warnings are ignored and cast aside when money or greed means more than people for those in leadership or positions of power? How many potentially catastrophic conditions are never brought to light?

Passage of a major infrastructure bill to repair worn bridges and roads that millions of Americans travel daily still faces hurdles in Congress. Sadly, if a major bridge collapses and there is loss of life, we cannot be sure that would have an impact. There are other regulatory bills stalled in Congress because the affected industries are lobbying against their passage. That is what happens when money or greed means more that the people to company executives. That is how the very people who are buying those companies' products and services are regarded.

The tragedy and tremendous loss of life in Surfside, Florida should be alarming to us all. It was a condominium complex there. A tragedy could occur in some other area of our lives tomorrow if and when money or greed means more than people by those in charge and who could prevent it. Where is the outrage, and calls to hold those accountable who are responsible?

Published June 27, 2021
https://janicesellis.com/blog

Interracial Dating and Marriage: Often Even Love Cannot Overcome Race and Racism

There is a refrain from an old love song, which goes: "Love and marriage, love and marriage go together like a horse and carriage...." What the song does not say is, "That depends...." Neither love nor marriage necessarily goes together if one of the two people comes from a different race or ethnic group.

While interracial marriages have increased since 1967 when a Supreme Court ruling overturned the right of states to enforce bans on interracial marriages, the vestiges of fear, ostracism, a discrimination of a different kind from family, friends, colleagues still reign larger than most of us might realize.

Findings from several recent opinion polls tell the story. One finding of the polls is consistent: The majority of Americans, about 63 percent, support interracial marriages. That number grows significantly, to over 84 percent when you ask younger people, 29 and under.

But when you examine the data a little closer and get into the details, a totally different picture emerges. This week on NPR (National Public Radio), it was revealed that today, 7.5 percent of all marriages in America are interracial. But race, and maybe racism, still plays a poignant role.

For example, of the interracial marriages: only 0.3 percent of white men are married to Black women; and just 0.8 white women are married to Black men. But contrast that with marriage among whites and other races or ethnic groups. For example: 2.1 percent or white men are married to Asian or Native American women; and 1.4 percent of white women are married to an Asian or Native American man.

While this may seem insignificant on the surface, a few conclusions are clear. There are more interracial marriages between Asian and whites than Blacks and whites even though there are millions of more marriages among Blacks than Asians.

Racial barriers are still a major factor among Blacks and whites when it comes to marriage, despite the fact that both groups support the idea. George Yancy, a sociologist at the University of North Texas, found in his research that only 6 in 10 Blacks compared to 8 in 10 Asians or Latinos are willing to date whites. Only 5 in 10 whites said they are willing to date Blacks, which is about the same as Blacks.

This sociologist, along with many of his colleagues, sees this as just one more hurdle to Blacks being able to successfully assimilate in American society compared to other races or ethnic groups—Asians, and Latinos for example. Harvard Sociologist, Orlando Patterson, notes that other minority groups gain great benefits through interracial marriage from exchanging and sharing child-rearing, to educational and cultural traditions.

Perhaps the most disturbing conclusion drawn from the data is that race is still more important than religion, politics, and occupational status when it comes to marriage.

It seems that love does not conquer all...

Published October 20, 2011
USAonRace.com

Is Racial Tension Increasing in America and Across the Globe?

Hardly a day goes by when there is not a report of some racially motivated incident. They often cut across age and socio-economic class. They are not confined to urban ghettos, but often include suburban neighborhoods, hamlets, and soccer fields and country clubs.

These incidents rarely make the evening news or the front pages of newspapers. But they beg for our attention, nonetheless.

Just this week alone, we have seen incidents of racial graffiti plastered on buildings on a university campus in Montana to the homes in New Hampshire. On Monday, student at the University of Montana found a white supremacy bumper sticker on the door of a Native American Center. Last week, discriminatory messages were stuffed into books in the African American section of the university's library.

In Concord, New Hampshire, the FBI has been called in to investigate three incidents of messages left on homes calling the families who lived in them "subhuman." The homes were those of African immigrants. On the positive side, white neighbors who were appalled at the messages helped to remove them.

But such incidents are not confined to the United States. In the United Kingdom, racist graffiti has been scrawled on the entrance of a beauty salon, adjacent to a welcome sign at a popular park. While these incidents targeted Blacks, the UK has found itself in the throes of racist comments against Indians and Asians. Most notably were the incidents that occurred at the polo club of which Prince Charles belongs.

Racial insensitivity has also played out on the cosmetic and confectionary stage, with companies recently pulling packaging and advertising that some groups found offensive.

Racial slurs are not confined to older generations who should know better. They pervade cyberspace where the very young dwells. The results of an Associated Press-MTV poll released this week show that teens and young adults often use and tolerate racial and derogatory names and slurs. While the young people acknowledge that use of such discriminatory words is wrong 54 percent still think it is fine to use them among friends.

The poll found that the derogatory language frequently used online by young people is not confined to racial groups, but such language is often used against women, gay people, and the obese.

Where do we break the cycle of wanton racial and social discrimination and insensitivity? Clearly, some incidents are blatant and in your face. But what about those that are just as pervasive in our communication media?

It is concerning to think that we are regressing, if not losing, the battle against creeping racism in all its forms and facets, across all races, black, white, brown, and beige. When we look at all the challenges we face as one humanity, we can ill afford to lose the war against racism.

Published September 22, 2011
USAonRace.com

Lessons We Humans Can Learn from Animals

We have all heard the saying, "They fight like cats and dogs." But there are lessons we humans can learn from animals. First, all cats and dogs do not fight each other. Many, if not most, get along just fine. Actually, our cat takes naps on our dog's face. However, that has not always been the case. One of our previous dogs found great pleasure in chasing and terrorizing one of our cats. So clearly, it all depends. But, depends on what?

One could speculate that maybe our current dog and cat get along swimmingly because they grew up together and shared their kitty and puppy days. That is partly the case. But the dog has also been accepting of older adopted cats that were complete strangers with different temperaments. There is no fighting, no chasing. They all get along. Lessons we humans can learn from animals—our cats and dogs for instance—are that they couldn't look more differently, and while growing up together or meeting as strangers, they still respect each other, live peaceably under the same roof, and often do things together.

We have a neighbor who loves animals, especially horses. On any given day when we pass by her farmhouse, it is not uncommon to see horses (large and miniature), donkeys, mules, sheep, goats, even peacocks, turkeys, and chickens of various breeds—all grazing and scratching alongside each other. We have yet to witness a dispute or scuffle between or among any of them during nearly two decades we have been neighbors. Plus, there are also dogs and cats. There are lessons we humans can learn from animals.

One could easily dismiss this example by saying, oh your neighbor operates a petting zoo, or she carefully picks docile animals. She does not. There could be another likely explanation. She loves animals. She shows it in her actions, her tone, her body language and how she cares for them and communicates with them. The animals see and feel her love, and they behave toward her and each other accordingly. Could those be the lessons we humans can learn from animals?

Several miles over as I was riding in the countryside, I looked over at a pasture with cows, Shetland ponies, elks, alpacas, and zebras. I thought to myself, what is it that we humans do not get? Those animals do not speak the same language, certainly do not look alike, and yet they all seem to get along.

This harmony, respect, and acceptance I just described among farm animals likely exist among many animals in the forests and jungles, even in the sea. Of course, there are those that do not get along, that prey on each other, and that live in fear of each other. But there are lessons we can learn from them, too. It is all about choice, training, exposure, acceptance, about how we choose to live with each other.

What lessons we humans can learn from animals!

Published April 16, 2021
https://janicesellis.com/blog

Knowing All the History of America

While there may be much to dread, much to regret, there is much more to gain in knowing all the history of America. How can the nation rid itself of systemic racism, inequality, injustices if it refuses to fully understand how and why we came to be where we are today? Why all the animus and objection to teaching "Critical Race Theory." How can we possibly believe that we will be able to make meaningful and lasting changes that are so sorely needed?

Not to fully acknowledge ALL of America's history—the good, the great, the bad, the despicable—is to forever operate in a false reality, to forever be sabotaged by the blind spots. We are only fooling ourselves to our detriment, thwarting what this nation can become and diminishing its march to real greatness. Knowing all the history of America can only lead to a better path forward.

You need not take my word for it. How many of you want to know the accurate and complete history of your family? What benefits do you gain? How does knowing your own history help you to chart a course for your life, whether it is the same or better? Knowing that history may not be all good. You may discover things that bring deep pain. The same is true with knowing all the history of America. So why all the fight against it?

What does denying it really gets us? Only temporal and temporary comfort. The adage that what is done in the dark will come to light rings true. It may take decades. It may take centuries.

But the truth will be revealed. We see instances of that all around us. Then why not be committed in knowing all the history of America, going forward. Why not include it in our history books, in the curricula being taught in our schools and higher institutions of learning. Sadly, that is not occurring at the level and the degree it should.

Look at the recent revelations about the experiences of Blacks brought to light by The New York Times 1619 Project and the Black Wall Street Massacre in Oklahoma to name a few. Look at the atrocities against Native Americans being brought to light by the discovery of mass grave sites in Kansas and Pennsylvania with the bodies of hundreds of Native American children. Yes, the atrocities and injustices perpetrated against Blacks and Native Americans are painful. They are ugly. Yet many of us would rather continue to bury our heads in the sand. We show little interest in knowing all of the history of America that allowed such inhumanity to occur.

Even worse yet, there are fights in the Halls of the United States Congress, in state legislatures, in our educational institutions and communities to stop and keep this side of American history in the dark, from being told. Is it just the name, "Critical Race Theory," that is causing such heart burn? Doubtful. The prospect of finally knowing all of American history is the real problem.

This denial and fear are grossly misplaced. Our ancestors were the perpetrators and victims alike. Hiding, omitting, and not knowing all the history of America has delayed and prevented efforts to put the nation on a healthy path when it comes to racial equality and overall healing.

While those egregious acts cannot be undone, we can neither absolve, totally insulate ourselves, nor live a life of detachment. So, why not acknowledge that those dreadful things indeed did happen, try to fix it. If not fix it, commit to charting a different path to stop the vestiges of those actions that still linger and cause grave harm today. That is what embracing and knowing all the history of America will do. Or, should do.

So, on with the efforts to have an accurate and complete accounting of American history. What kind of future is in store for this country if we do not?

Published November 7, 2021
https://janicesellis.com/blog

Lessons of African American History: Closing the Racial Divide

February is Black History month, and it presents an educational opportunity that can aid us in closing the great racial divide between Blacks and whites.

Designating February as Black History month is the nation's attempt to correct its lack of acknowledgement and treatment of African Americans in the normal annals of America's history. While it is a good remedial effort, the month-long recognition is not enough within itself.

The best solution will occur only when it is no longer necessary to set aside a month to note the significant achievements of a particular race or ethnic group. A time when the rewriting of new editions of the history books reflects a truly accurate historical account of advances in the arts, sciences, politics, business, and every other subject area where Americans, irrespective of their race, ethnic or religious origins, contributed with distinction.

However, until that time, it is incumbent on all of us to continue to do what is necessary to not only set the record straight, but also foster the kind of dialogue to further enlighten us, and more importantly, our children.

Although we have made great progress, we still have many areas where we must seek further enlightenment to improve our understanding of each other. Nevertheless, too often, rather than explore some of those areas—albeit many of them uncomfortable and disconcerting—we are far more comfortable allowing a label or stereotypical view to be the prism through which we see each other. Even worse, we tend to apply those views to an entire race of people.

Since the mid-term elections will occur this year and the Republicans and Democrats are already in a fierce battle to keep or gain legislative seats, I thought I might attempt to provide a little enlightenment around our two-party system of government, and how a lack of understanding of our true history could forever keep up in the dark.

Take the prevalent view that most Blacks are more liberal than conservative and therefore are, or should, belong to the Democratic Party rather than the Republican Party. Along with that view are other philosophical assumptions that come into play. On the individual level, there is a prevalent belief that most Black people believe in big government programs rather than economic self-sufficiency. On the organizational level, there is the belief that the Democratic Party is more inclusive, empathetic, and supportive of the needs and interests of Blacks than the Republican Party.

I am sure just those two notions could stir heated debate in many circles. However, past, and recent history could provide interesting facts to engage the discussion. For example, did you know, that following the Civil War and during Reconstruction, Blacks were very active in Republican Party politics and served in almost every level of government?

For more than a decade, Blacks held offices from the United States Congress—there were two senators and fourteen representatives—to state legislatures, city councils and county commissions. Blacks held more offices in the Deep South than any place else. Throughout that period, these remarkable individuals held the majority in the House of Representatives for the state of South Carolina. A state that is remembered today for having vehemently fought to continue to fly the confederate flag atop its capitol and having a representative of this state make history by calling President Barrack Obama a liar during an address to Congress for all the world to hear.

Many of these historical political advances for Blacks were a direct result of the Abolitionist Movement. One of its strongest and most effective leaders was Frederick Douglass, a black man, who remained a staunch Republican all of his life. Douglass, described as an indefatigable journalist, and influential orator in great demand, held a number of positions in the national government.

Since that period, there have not been two black US senators simultaneously serving in either party, or Black people certainly do not form a majority in any state's legislature. The reasons are subjects whose treatment could fill much more space than is available here. Nevertheless, the discussion is certainly worth having by civic-minded Blacks and whites interested in making a two-party system work better for all groups.

More importantly, such a discussion could go a long way to dispel some myths that are at a minimum negatively compromising, if not downright regressive, in the century-old quest for Black people to exercise their political power and influence to advance their interest just like other ethnic groups.

Some good results could emerge. Among them, the realization that Blacks, like whites, are both liberal and conservative; most blacks would prefer a meaningful wage-earning job than welfare; and we all share the same loathsome regard for paying excessive taxes.

However, perhaps the greatest realization of all would be for more Blacks and whites to recognize the importance of participating in a significant way in both parties to affect those issues that are important to them on an ongoing basis.

If that were the case, neither party would take such a large voting constituency for granted or totally ignore it during election time. Moreover, irrespective of what party is in power, Blacks, like Hispanics, Jews, and other ethnic groups, could have a significant number of seats at the legislative tables.

Frederick Douglass and the Reconstruction era taught us that.

Published February 1, 2010
USAonRace.com

Life of Martin Luther King, Jr. Is An Example

If you ever doubt that one person can make a difference, the life of Martin Luther King, Jr. is an example that we should never forget. Too often, we see a problem, an injustice, a need of any kind and feel we are helpless to do anything about it.

When confronted with a situation that needs a voice or action, we allow those feelings of helplessness and doubt to take over. We are besieged by questions like: Who am I? What can I do? Too often, we conclude we are powerless to do anything.

The life of Martin Luther King, Jr. is an example of how not to let those feelings of doubt and helplessness deter you. In the face of fear and constant threats of harm and death, Martin Luther King, Jr. refused to be deterred from his work to achieve racial and social justice.

As we reflect on the life of Martin Luther King, Jr., we should be inspired to become engaged and involved with whatever issues or conditions concern us. As we pause to commemorate the birthday of King, the only question is: Do we care as much as he did? This is a question we should ask ourselves every day, at every opportunity.

There is no greater force or power than that of the human will. We see it all around. We see it in extraordinary athletic achievements in sports. We see it in the awesome achievements of those with physical or mental disabilities.

And then, there are those who have achieved incredible gains for others who have suffered physical oppression, social inequality, economic and judicial injustices, across generations for centuries. The life of Martin Luther King, Jr. is an example of one of those giants.

It should be noted that King was a teenager when he became interested in getting rid of racial injustice in America. It was an interest that turned into a mission—a mission that he pursued during his entire short life, a mission that costs him his life. Had he not died at the hand of an assassin and lived, we would be celebrating his 91st birthday!

When he felt compelled to fight to improve the plight of the oppressed, he did not know all the things he would confront. But, during the days, weeks, months, and years, he stayed the course despite constant obstacles, threats, persecution, and physical and emotional abuse.

The life of Martin Luther King, Jr. is an example, which shows if you care enough, are bold enough, courageous enough, and believe enough, you can make a difference.

As we pause to commemorate Dr. King, each of us can give serious thought about how we can apply our efforts to make things better wherever we can, as Martin Luther King, Jr. did.

Published January 17, 2020
https://janicesellis.com/blog

Longing For the Lessons of Horatio Alger

Horatio Alger, most assuredly, is turning over in his grave with the "rags-to-riches" rise of the executives of some of the nation's largest corporations and the greedy, fraudulent and pernicious way in which they have gotten there.

Alger, certainly, cannot be resting in peace.

Alger, during the post-Civil War era, wrote over a hundred books extolling the virtue of hard work, perseverance, and honesty. The heroes of his books had strong ethical and moral values. They exhibited kindness and generosity on their road to success.

Even though more that 250 million copies of his books have been sold worldwide, perhaps a few of them need to be required reading for present and future executives and the boards that are responsible for governing them.

A few relevant books for the times in which we find ourselves come to mind *Fame and Fortune, Ragged Dick, Risen from the Ranks, Brave and Bold, and Abraham Lincoln.*

Alger's books really have lessons for us all. And it may be well for our lawmakers to dust off a few of his books and read them for moral strength as they deliberate about what is the appropriate punishment for corporate thievery.

Despite this election year, perhaps, they themselves will exercise moral courage with the enforcement of strong laws that will mete out the right punishment for the crimes that have been perpetrated against ordinary and trusting citizens—many of whom still believe in the Horatio Alger way of doing things.

As we assess the candidates running for elective office, we need to ask the question, "What will you do to ensure that employees, investors and their families are not exploited by illegal and unscrupulous business practices?" And we need to listen very carefully to the answers.

In the short term, not only has unsuspecting older Americans been robbed of hard-earned money they had depended on for retirement, but other workers have seen college funds for their kids dissipate. Money saved to buy their first home evaporated.

If our President and members of Congress fail to do the right thing, it could seriously undermine not only our free enterprise way of life, but it could also mortgage our future because young people who are watching may find it difficult to continue to believe in some of the fundamental tenets that keep our Republic strong.

And no matter how many Horatio Alger books they read, they may easily conclude that they refer to a bygone way of life, with characters whose belief systems and moral values no longer are applicable in a business world that seem devoid of them.

What a tragedy, should this occur.

Each year, the Horatio Alger Association of Distinguished Americans host an annual awards dinner in our nation's capital. The Horatio Alger Award is given to ten Americans who have made outstanding contributions in their fields. Since its inception in 1947, many elected officials and business have been honored.

The Association offers many programs to bring together Horatio Alger heroes of today with those of tomorrow. Young people are offered opportunities to explore firsthand how America's free enterprise system works. During the National Scholars Conference, which is held in Washington, D.C., students are able to see how our executive, legislative and judicial branches of government work.

If we have not had a near melt-down of our economic infrastructure, participant in future Horatio Alger conferences will have much to discuss and many lessons to learn. If our elected official and justice system have done their jobs, hopefully the real corporate crooks will be in jail and systems will be in place to make it difficult for those who are so criminally inclined to run amok again.

It would do us well to perhaps hold Horatio Alger workshops for young people all across America to teach them what constitutes a good code of business conduct. To remind them that despite what they see in many of the corporate leaders, there is a right and decent way to go from "rags-to-riches" and it is not always about how much personal wealth you amass. It also involves how you help and enrich the lives of others.

There are many elected officials and business leaders who exemplify the very values and that needs to be passed on to future generations.

Will the Horatio Alger Distinguished Americans please stand up?

Published July 12, 2002
The Kansas City Star

President Barack Obama's Message to Activists

President Barack Obama's message to activists is one that can be applied across race and ethnicity, for all who speak, act and work for a cause. His message for the ages, and for all of us who have causes we care about, was delivered during his commencement address to graduates of Howard University.

While Obama spoke to a predominately black graduating class at one of the nation's oldest Historically Black Colleges and Universities, there is great advice for those of us who fashion ourselves to be activists in words or actions, and who have been at it all our lives or just beginning. Obama's message to activists resonates.

In his remarks, Obama acknowledged, and urged the young graduates to also acknowledge, how far America has come in the last fifty years in many areas. One of the areas he noted was race relations. There are signs all around: More African Americans are graduating from high school; many more are earning college degrees; there are more black elected officials at every level of government; Blacks are senior executives and CEOs of major corporations.

But with this progress, Obama readily acknowledged that America still has a long way to go. Racism and inequality still persist. There are still efforts to deny or make it harder to vote. The justice system still greatly discriminates against young Blacks and other minorities.

There are socioeconomic gaps and poverty that affect Blacks and whites. While the economy is improving, many people are still hurting and finding it very difficult to make ends meet. Obama's message to activists, which he indicated those graduates could choose to become, made it clear that there is so much still to be done to make life in America better.

For those in that graduating class or those of us who want to help address these challenges moving forward, Obama's message made it clear that there are things that we must do to be effective.

Obama's message to activists.

First, we need to be confident in who we are, whether you are black, white, Hispanic, Asian, whatever your race or ethnicity.

Second, we need to be acutely aware of our history, our struggle. No one can meet the world in ignorance or with a sense of entitlement. You must understand the other person's perspective, fight, and work hard to find common ground and a path to meaningful change.

Third, we not only need passion about a cause but a strategy that can be put into action, which might include not just creating awareness, but mobilizing votes and other actions on every level, all the time.

And fourth, you can just speak out. You must listen as well, especially to those with whom you disagree. You will not effectively implement your strategy without understanding the opposition.

All activists must realize that progress requires building allies, making compromises, and staying the course. You commit yourself to a cause that is bigger than yourself and you work at it, in some way, every day. It often takes years and decades to realize meaningful change. All we have to do is look at history and the activists who have gone before us.

If we remember Obama's message to activists, we can remain motivated when times are tough, when progress seems to be out of reach, and we feel like throwing up our hands. We need to remain confident in who we are, know our history, execute our strategy and be willing to listen to the opposition. That is Obama's message to activists. And what a great message to keep.

Published May 12, 2016
https://janicesellis.com/blog

One Community, One Defense

The ties that bind. Sometimes, it is amazing what it takes for different people from different walks of life to recognize the things they have in common—the things that bind them. To finally recognize that differences in skin color may not be the great divide we think it is. But, rather, other things like religion, economic disparity, a way of life build the greatest chasms.

If September 11, 2001 did nothing else, it signaled to all Americans, irrespective of our race, ethnicity, religion, or dwelling place—urban, suburban, or rural—that we were equally disliked and disregarded in the eyes of terrorists who hate everything about our democratic way of life. We suddenly became one, united in our patriotic feelings and the desire to protect America and our way of life irrespective of its imperfections.

September 11 also changed our lives forever. As much as we may note the change, the implications for the lifestyles of future generations are tremendously significant. Our children and grandchildren may never know the sense of peace and security that America provided us and our forefathers. Proclaiming children are our future, our most valuable resource, has become a common and frequent refrain. But the gravity of its meaning has never loomed larger than it does today as we face, perhaps, the war of all wars.

The never-ending war against terrorism in all its facets—chemical, biological, dirty bombs and all—is likely to be long fought and potentially could claim many lives in its wake. Any LASTING victory against terrorism will be directly dependent on how well we, first, protect our children and then prepare them to fight it—beginning yesterday.

Terrorism, in all its facets, is a cruel and cowardice. We have become all too familiar with many of its methods, as we have seen the devastation of car bombs exploding on crowded streets, truck bombs careening into occupied buildings. And we shall never forget hijacked planes being used as deadly missiles.

But bioterrorism (the release of deadly germs and chemicals) is one of the most vicious and insidious facets of this kind of war. The deadliest weapons used are often cloaked in familiar disguise or undetectable at all. And even when detected, they could be untreatable. So, it is a tougher weapon to disarm, destroy or neutralize.

More disturbingly, bioterrorism is a weapon of war that puts our children most at risk in the short term and over a protracted period of time. They are vulnerable on multiple fronts: physically, emotionally, and educationally. Our children could become the largest casualties of war—both immediate and long-term.

While we are here and in charge, to some degree we can protect and preserve their way of life. But even so, that will not be easy. For example: On the physical front, health care professionals are ill prepared to diagnose or treat victims of a chemical or biological attack, particularly on a large scale and one involving children.

Long after the September 11 attack, pediatricians were voicing concern about the potential loss of life among children if there is a widespread outbreak of anthrax, smallpox, or a release of poisonous gas. The lack of information, treatment protocols and appropriates drug therapy for children were a widespread concern. Developing effective means to protect the physical health of our children must become a high priority in any homeland defense strategy at the national and local level. We may not have the luxury of unlimited time.

On the emotional front, we all, from time to time, find ourselves, reeling. Many adults are still finding it difficult to make sense of it all. Imagine what children must be feeling: overwhelming fear, insecurity, sadness, helplessness. Psychologists and other childcare professionals are advising us, as parents, teachers, mentors, and caring adults, of the importance of spending time with our children.

On the educational front, there are short and long-term issues that must be addressed if our kids are to win the fight against all facets of terrorism. On an individual level, we must help them better understand different cultures and religions and why they may or may not be accepting of the American way of life.

On a broader and lasting scale, terrorism will not be understood and defeated until we ensure we are closing the illiteracy gap that exist among the majority of kids in the areas of the social, biological, and chemical sciences. We know in Missouri, for example, that most of our high school students are not meeting the minimum competency standards in these subjects.

The nation has major challenges in closing the achievement gap in many subjects. Until we effectively address this major weakness in our armory, how can we expect our children to become the physicists, chemists, geneticists, physicians, social scientists, historians and educated citizenry that it will take to wage and win wars of the 21st century?

The lasting victory over terrorism will be won not only on foreign soil, but also when we have protected and prepared our children on multiple fronts, here at home. As we approach the anniversary of that life-altering and historic day, September 11, one of the most important challenges we face is: How do we prepare our children to take care of themselves and thrive in a changing world, a changing America?

Published September 6, 2002
The Kansas City Star

Our Love Hate Relationship with Color

Imagine living in a colorless world. How dull, boring, downright morose, that would be.

Color, in all of its variety, is considered one of the spices of life. It excites and stimulates the imagination. Painters and photographers capture it on canvass. Poets and pundits describe it on the printed page.

We marvel at nature's awesome beauty and bounty displayed by its parade of color as we enjoy the flowers of spring and summer, the maple trees and evergreens in fall and winter. And need we mention furnishings and fashions, works of art, and yes, body art.

But color takes on a whole different meaning when it is associated with race, people of different hues and shades.

As we celebrate the birthday of Martin Luther King Jr., it would be good to ponder the human condition he, and so many others before him, fought and paid the ultimate sacrifice to change—the ugliness, the discrimination, the injustice, the persecution perpetrated upon fellow human beings because of differences in color.

Color in all of its richness seems to be welcome in many, if not every, aspect of our lives except when it comes to other human beings—of color, that is. When it comes to people, suddenly different colors and shades provoke closed mindedness rather than openness, fear rather than friendliness, oppression rather than freedom, and the baseness within us rather than the beautiful.

Our schizophrenic relationship with the notion of color is an age-old one. We love it in things. We loathe it in human beings. History is replete with examples of our worse behavior toward other human beings who do not look like us, dress like us, talk like us, worship like us, live like us.

Today, little has changed when we look in some urban and rural areas in this country and many other places around the world.

Imagine the possibilities if we could appreciate the richness of diversity in people of different colors as we appreciate those in nature, and our own creations.

Imagine if we could afford the same respect to peoples' differences, and yet find greater understanding of ourselves, of others, of the world and our place in it.

Imagine if we could believe that every child, black, white, brown or yellow has the same needs: caring parents, safe neighborhoods, good schools, an opportunity to dream and to become whatever they dream of becoming.

Imagine if it could become natural, a matter of unconscious practice, that every human being is given the benefit of the doubt and treated equally when he or she applies for a job, submits an application for college, goes to buy a house or rent an apartment.

If different colors in people could be regarded with the same reverence and respect as that in nature, there would be no need for affirmative action, equal rights and equal employment protection, fair housing and other laws just to get us to do the right thing toward each other.

Just imagine how better off we would be if we could accept the diversity in color among us as people as comfortably, as eagerly, as expectantly as we do in nature and in our surroundings,

The economic, social and educational cast systems created around color and because of color have done as much to imprison and deprive the perpetrators as the perpetrated.

There will be many multi-racial gatherings across the country this week—Kansas City's among the largest—to celebrate the birthday of Martin Luther King, Jr. and his life's fight against racial injustices, those inequities, misdeeds, even criminal behavior born of differences in color.

Perhaps a lasting tribute to King is to take time and get in touch with our conflicting feelings around color.

Perhaps the first place to begin is with the simple acknowledgment of the common color that binds us all, the color that runs in all of our veins, that fulfills the same purpose—the gift of life. That color and its purpose are undeniable.

When will we cease to allow the insignificant differences in skin color to confuse and compromise the quality of life we could share as neighbors, colleagues, fellow travelers on the world stage?

Isn't that the only lasting celebration?

Published January 9, 2001
The Kansas City Star

Waging a Protracted War on Terrorism

Are we, the current generations of Americans like the generations before us, prepared for "The War of the 21st Century?" President Obama, Congress, our troops, our nation will need support from all of us.

Despite the official withdrawal of American troops from Iraq signifying an end to active military engagement, we still have Afghanistan and other watch points. The war on terrorism will be a different war. It will be a long-fought war. It is a war that will require an attack on multiple fronts, using multiple strategies to destroy an enemy with multiple disguises and scattered in many places.

But are the "baby-boom" and the "X" and "Y" generations psychologically prepared for the full ramifications of a far-reaching protracted war? Are we prepared to make sacrifices on a scale we thought we would never have to make, possibly sending tens of thousands of our sons and daughters to war, year after year? Will we be willing to relinquish many aspects of individual freedom that we have zealously guarded, vigorously debated? Are we prepared to accept more death and destruction on our soil? Even those, that today, we may be unable to fathom.

We have intermittent anger, angst, and concern. *But will we hold together for the long haul?*

These are questions not to be taken lightly.

I vividly remember the gut-wrenching experience at the bus station when my family sent a son and brother to the Vietnam War, and the many horrid days during the long two years that he served. I often recall those gripping feelings of uncertainty when the son of that Vietnam veteran, my nephew, was sent to fight in Desert Storm.

But irrespective of our personal experiences with previous wars, the "baby-boom" and "X" and "Y" generations bring a different collective psyche to the challenge.

First, our generations will go into a war with the realization that a foreign force was able to execute 9/11, a surprise attack that wrought unprecedented devastation on the continental United States, piercing that precious veil of safety and security we have so long enjoyed. The sense of having an impenetrable wall of protection is no more. The terrorist attacks and attempted attacks that have occurred as we close this first decade of the 21st century have not helped.

Yes, the attack on Pearl Harbor on December 7, 1941 was surprising to Americans but not as devastating as 9/11 and its aftermath. Pearl Harbor also occurred almost two years after World War II had begun and most of Europe had become engaged. My father, a World War II Navy veteran, often recalled how our parents and grandparents had a sense that ultimately, the odds were, the United States would also be drawn into the war. Furthermore, the end of World War I was hardly twenty years removed.

The baby boomers are a generation whose sons and daughters have not been exposed or subjected to being drafted and required to serve in the armed forces. I remember the discussion in our household when my youngest brother decided to join the Marines. A 21-year veteran Marine, he now calls to put in perspective the likelihood of our grandsons and granddaughters being called or volunteering to fight the war on terrorism.

Our grandfathers and fathers who fought in both world wars and the Korean War, and our husbands and brothers who fought in the Vietnam War grew up with a sense of obligation to serve and protect their country. A sense of patriotism and duty was ingrained in them.

Whether they wanted to or not, whether they agreed with the premises of war or not, being committed to defend America and all it stood for was not a voluntary option.

Communism was the enemy then. Terrorism is the enemy now.

Despite years of terrorist attacks in other parts of the world, contemporary Americans have lived with the unswerving belief that we were insulated from the menacing forces that other countries face every day.

As a result of 9/11, and other attempts, on its own soil, America must now take the lead and shoulder the greatest responsibility for this war, with or without all allies lined up with us.

How do we, the baby-boom generation and the X and Y generations, achieve the best state of readiness in the months and years ahead to be victorious in what portends to be a protracted war? We must:

- Be united as a nation, supporting our leaders and our troops as they make the best decisions and execute the best strategies
- Be vigilant, very vigilant, about our encounters and our environment since there are enemies among us preparing to carry out a terrorist act against us
- Educate our children and youth on the nature and consequences of war, explaining to them how religious, racial, and cultural intolerance can bring out the worse in human behavior, and how we all have an enduring obligation in defeating it
- Lead the way, doing everything within our individual and collective capacity to ensure that history will judge our response and performance to be among our finest in defending democracy and the values we hold so dear

Generations did it before us. We must do it for the generations to follow.

Fighting terrorism is our generations' war.

Published September 3, 2010
USAonRace.com

Public Must Require Consistent Laws to Address Crimes of the Church

Separation of church and state—the leadership of the Catholic Church seems to have taken it literally, and an untold number of children have suffered life-altering consequences because of it.

The recent revelations, one after the other, of priests having a history of sexually molesting young boys as they moved from one parish to the other, are extremely disturbing. But to have the bishops and cardinals take the law into their own hands and mete out their own form of justice is even more atrocious.

It seems in more instances than not, the offending priest with or without rehabilitation, was issued a reprieve and opportunity to go and not only sin no more, but instead live to break the law, another day. An opportunity to abuse an unsuspecting, vulnerable child.

If a young boy cannot find a safe refuge in the church, where is protection to be found?

This is not an indictment of all priests in every Catholic Church. Nor is it a formal accusation of all bishops and cardinals who take the law into their own hands, meting out justice, when it comes to crimes committed by their own.

Leaders in other religious faiths are not without their own sins and brushes with the law whether they were found committing adultery with a member of their church or a prostitute, or taking money designated for advancing the ministry and lining their own pockets instead.

You may recall the fall of TV evangelists, Jimmy Swaggart, Jim and Tammy Baker. You may recall Jim Baker served time in prison for one of his misdeeds, embezzling funds. So, did Henry Lyons, the president of the National Baptist Convention, for the same crime. The laws and penalties regarding embezzlement are clear.

While one would hope that church leadership would do the morally and legally correct thing, perhaps the law, or the lack there of, has been aiding and abetting these criminal acts of child abuse and molestation by priests.

Most states do not require the clergy to report abuse. Apparently, only twelve states specifically require the clergy to report suspected abuse. Another sixteen states have laws with language requiring anyone to report any knowledge of abuse.

Missouri and Kansas are among the states with no laws requiring clergy to report suspected child abuse. We have work to do when both legislative bodies convene their session next year. But what do we do in the meantime? The recent action of a local priest makes it abundantly clear we need to do something.

With all the media coverage about the alleged abuse by priests in Boston, and former priest from Missouri and Kansas, it was reported in the *Kansas City Star* last Tuesday that an associate priest at a Roman Catholic Church in Lenexa recently instructed parishioners to report any child abuse, attempted or committed by a priest, to the archbishop, not the police or any legal authority.

The associate priest made it clear that any decisions regarding the priest's actions resided solely with the archbishop. He further urged that it was the parishioners' duty to be kind and merciful, willingly forgiving the offending priest. The associate priest failed to outline the duty of the offending priest.

The presiding priest at the church in Lenexa has rushed to correct the position of the associate priest. But it begs the question why the associate priest felt comfortable making such statements in the first place.

But this local priest's attitude and position are not in isolation. Despite the continuing revelations of priest who have, or are alleged to have, sexually abused young boys, the leadership of the Catholic Church still seems reluctant to come forth and support and submit to stronger laws that govern the laity.

Just recently, the Survivors Network of Those Abused by Priest urged Roman Catholic bishops to assist with passing legislation in every state that would require church officials to report suspected abuse, and the prosecution of priests who were accused of abuse. The bishops had no comment in reference to the request.

The public must intervene swiftly, and decisively to help the church regain its moral compass and moral authority. It is teetering through its silence, and when speaking, its weak resolve.

There is little that can be done for the unknown number of children, young boys, who have suffered at the hands of those who should have been the trust worthiest, their priests. There may be other instances of child abuse in other denominations and faiths.

In addition to giving them all the therapy and support they need, the best thing we can do is enact laws that will at least, at a minimum, serve as a deterrent, and at most meet out swift justice.

That is the least we can do. Let us begin with getting those laws on the books in Kansas and Missouri. We owe it to our children, those who are affected and those who are watching.

Published May 20, 2002
The Kansas City Star

Should Race Relations Have a Slot on the Evening News Just as Sports or Weather?

When will we get the courage to confront racism in our communities and the commitment to really do something about it? Until race relations become a part of the local and national dialogue as sports, the weather or other things we talk about on a daily basis, we will forever be content to just show outrage as ugly incidents continue to occur.

Yes, there is coverage of high-profile acts that seem to be racially motivated. We all remember the Trayvon Martin killing in Florida, which was the center of demonstrations, hearings, and television talk shows for weeks on end. The upcoming trial of George Zimmerman, the shooter, will undoubtedly have a spot on the Evening News until the verdict is rendered.

Even after the trial is over and whether the findings determine that it was an incident of racial profiling, brandishing want-to-be police power, raw testosterone unleashed, or a combination thereof, the Trayvon Martin-George Zimmerman incident and its aftermath implore more questions that need honest and open discussion.

How can that conversation occur in family rooms, around the dinner table, in cafes and clubs if we are to move beyond the labeling and stop falling into the same old perennial cycle of accusation and denial?

How does America have an honest and sustained conversation about how race plays in our everyday lives?

Again, many of us likely remember the wanton killing of a Muslim mother of five in California. The killer or killers left a calling card imploring the family to get out of America.

Then, there was the senseless killing of a black man in Mississippi who happened to be walking to a convenience store when he was beaten and run over by a pick-up truck driven by white teens who were looking to kill a "Nigger." They found an innocent unsuspecting black man and killed him.

But, what about all the low-profile incidents, those that do not make national news, that are occurring on a daily basis in communities all across America, involving people of all racial and ethnic groups?

An overriding question: Why do we continually avoid confronting matters of race that is such a part of our daily lives—in blatant and subliminal ways?

Until we are willing to take inventory on an individual, group, and societal level, of all those factors—factual and fictional—that shape our attitudes and actions as we interact with others who are different from ourselves, race will continue to be used as a divisive and destructive force.

Incidents that would otherwise be considered as everyday encounters and common conflicts take on a life of their own, fueled by the stereotypes and labels that we hang on to and allow to order our world view. Do we care whether they are accurate or inaccurate? Are we afraid to examine their veracity, for fear it might lead us out of our comfort zone, shatter the monochromatic world to which we predictably retreat?

Do we really believe we have more to gain by remaining cloistered and close-minded than seeking the truth about others unlike ourselves? What about the enlightenment and richness that awaits us if we break through the blinders of racial bigotry on all sides?

How many more killings and ugly incidents will it take for us to finally get to the heart of the matter: stop jumping the gun, stop over- or under- reacting, stop retreating or raging, stop denying or over-compensating, stop being reticent or overly eager—just stop the extremes when it comes to race. Until our extreme reactions cease, normalcy, in all its meaning, will continue to elude us as a society.

But how do we get there? Who owns the conversations and actions to bring about meaningful change? We all do.

Wouldn't it be grand if communities all across America held townhall meetings and forums on racial issues just as they do on educational issues, taxes, and other public policies?

Wouldn't it be grand if the morning and evening news shows had a daily and regular segment in their programming on race relations right along with the segments on sports or the weather? Shouldn't matters of race be just as important?

Real improvement in race relations begins and grows with how we think, act, and react in our daily encounters.

Until racial diversity is as normal and as American as apple pie, we have a long way to go, and we need to be about it with every opportunity in aspects of our daily lives.

What do you think?

Published November 29, 2012
USAonRace.com

Racial Biases Infecting the Doctor's Office

Misperceptions, attitudes, biases, and stereotypes about race, whether consciously or subconsciously have a negative impact on the doctor-patient relationship and therefore could adversely affect the quality of health care provided and the corresponding outcomes.

The findings of a new study, just released by John Hopkins Medicine, provide evidence that racial biases and stereotypical views, whether overt or not, influence what and how health care is delivered. There is also evidence that such prejudicial attitudes could be a direct cause of the disparities among races perpetuated in health care settings across the United States.

The report is published in the *American Journal of Public Health*. The lead researcher in the study, Dr. Lisa Cooper, notes, "If patients have good patient-centered interactions with their doctors, we know they're more likely to follow through with care, make follow-up appointments and better control diseases such as diabetes and depression. This study suggests that unconscious racial attitudes may be standing in the way of positive interactions to the detriment of patient health."

What is really compelling about the findings of the study is that it was conducted with primary care physicians and patients who knew each other well and had a relationship over time. The physicians had agreed to participate in the study to improve the care provided to African American patients and were willing to take pretests to determine racial biases and to have subsequent patient visits recorded.

The findings are concerning. Researchers found that white and Asian physicians held more positive attitudes toward white patients than black patients when it comes to who is more compliant with medical advice. Black physicians had more neutral attitudes.

Researchers also found evidence of a direct correlation between racial attitudes, communication during a visit and the patient's perception of the quality of their experience during the visit. Primary care physicians with racial biases or stereotypical views tended to talk more than listen during the visit with a black patient; and tended to spend less time addressing the emotional and psychological aspects of the illness and any treatment challenges that patient might be having.

As a result, black patients often leave their doctor's offices feeling disrespected, having lower levels of trust and confidence in their physician, and feeling they are not involved in their treatment options or decisions.

The researchers acknowledge that progress has been made in society generally when it comes to being more open to and accepting of different races and ethnicities.

"But we have subconscious bias that we develop from our earliest experiences and are less subject to social pressures," says Dr. Cooper.

But John Hopkins, Dr. Cooper, the team of researcher, the participating primary care physicians, and their patients should be commended for being willing to confront the issue of overt and subliminal racial attitudes and biases. Being willing to face those negative realities is the first step to making necessary improvements that can bring about needed change on everyone's part.

Achieving the best health outcomes, after all, is what the patient and doctor hold in common irrespective of race or ethnicity. Dr. Cooper poignantly captures it when she says, "If we are more aware of how our attitudes are affecting our behaviors, only then can we change what we do and ensure that all of our patients get the best care."

There are many other professions that could learn a lesson from this study.

Published March 20, 2012
USAonRace.com

Random and Racist Acts of Violence

We, as Americans, must come to terms with both random and racist acts of violence. Instances of both types of pernicious and pre-meditated crimes against humanity occur all too often in what purports to be one of the most civilized societies.

How have we gone so far astray? How is that civility and reason are not screaming in our collective conscience that we have to get at the root causes of random and racist acts of violence?

We must begin by getting rid of the "straw men" in the quest to find meaningful solutions. Stopping random and racist acts of violence are not about law-abiding citizens being indiscriminately denied their 2nd Amendment Rights afforded by the Constitution to bear arms to protect one's property. It is not just the deranged or the demonic that wield high powered weapons against the unsuspecting innocents, or hyperbolic hate-filled rhetoric followed by heinous acts waged against a racial or ethnic groups.

It is time to fess up America. It is much more than one or the other of the above.

Reducing gun violence is a complex issue that will require rational discussion on multiple fronts: Guns easily accessible to the mentally ill and the hate-filled; laws on the books that are ignored or loosely enforced.

Does it mean anything that America is the most violent industrialized nation on the planet? We have more murders per capita, and more incidents like those in Tucson, Aurora, Oak Creek, Newtown, and other places, unfortunately yet to be named, than any other modern civilization.

Do we not care about the random and racist acts of violence that have occurred and those that are being planned or perpetrated?

The Associated Press just reported an incident in Montgomery, Alabama that was foiled before more lives were taken. Apparently, an Alabama teenager who described himself as a white supremacist made journal entries about a plot to bomb classmates three days after the Newtown school massacre and began building small homemade explosives. It is believed that the school shootings in Newtown influenced this would be killer.

The teen told investigators that he is a white supremacist, explaining why five of the six students he named in his journal as targets are black. A vigilant teacher found the journal and turned it over to authorities. The teen also indicated using firearms, which several were found in the home.

This potential tragedy was averted. But how many more will not be detected. Have we become a nation that is only motivated by the drama or outrage of the day or week, but fall back into our complacent and complicit state as times goes by, as our sensitivity and outrage lessen?

Is this how a civilized, otherwise reasoning, people deal with the mental health issues, vigilantes, loose laws, and fear-mongering demagogues in addressing this most serious issue of gun violence?

Random and racist violence has no place in a caring and civilized society. In not becoming engaged in seeking solutions, we are all guilty. We are all responsible.

Published January 7, 2013
USAonRace.com

Reigning In Capitalism's Ugly Side–Unchecked Greed

Strong laws and regulations, with proactive compliance reviews with stiff penalties for gross business violations, are the best defenses against the unseemly side of our free market system. *If* only they were diligently enforced.

Let us hope that as the United States Senate debates the issues around financial reform that they will be ever mindful of the great elephant on the floor—wanton greed and make sure the appropriate checks and balances are part of the bill that finally passes into law.

We have had several poignant examples of greed gone awry. Remember the melt-down of energy giant, Enron? Seems like a long time ago. But that was just the tip of the financial corruption iceberg.

In the last year alone, we have had a number of long-standing and trusted financial giants melt down and be rescued by governmental tax dollars only to see the executives of those same companies pay themselves big bonuses as if they had kept the company afloat and had a profitable year.

As the growing allegations at Goldman Sachs unfold—descriptions of high rolling, risk taking executives who created and cashed-in on investment deals that they bet against—the tentacles of that scandal could reach so far that, by the time the investigation is complete, public confidence may never be the same.

It begs the question how many more—large, medium, or small—are out there, taking advantage of the trusting consumer, financially and otherwise, all in the name of monetary gain.

Examples abound.

We have seen businesses take advantage of a community's welcome mat by polluting their soil and water supply with chemicals that are known detriments to human health. On any given week on the evening news or in the local newspaper, we see the emergence of illnesses, cancer in particular, at a rate which is disproportionate to a community's size. How can we help but wonder what other environmental and health risks there are in communities across America that may not come to light until there is a catastrophe?

How pervasive is unchecked greed in our free-market society? It seems to have no respect of persons living or dead. Remember the recent case in Chicago, where the same burial plots were sold to multiple people? The investigation revealed multiple human remains were piled in a mass grave. Was the thought, "Let us make as much money on this plot as we can? Bury. Dig up. And bury again." A similar story occurred in northwest Georgia a few years ago. Hundreds of human remains that should have been cremated as far back as 15 years previously have been found in bags, dumped, and strewn near and around the grounds of the crematory. Yet another example of unlawful business practices gone unnoticed for a long period of time.

And then there is the issue of immigration, particularly undocumented workers from Mexico. Could it be that capitalism's ugly side is intertwined in that issue as well? Does it come right down to the profit motive once again? Getting cheap labor, avoiding the costs associated with legitimate employees will all improve the bottom line—and year-end bonuses.

Are we at last ready to deal with the hypocrisy around the real reason we do not want to even enforce the immigration laws on the books?

It will do us well to examine what has emerged over the years as the definition of business success, which is more money, more money, and more money. Large and sustained profit margins rule the daily dealings. It seems that the basic tenant of a free market capitalistic society has become bastardized with the craze to increase profits. Sometimes at any cost.

Capitalism is not about how much money you can make by taking advantage of the unsuspecting or the weak. What is often forgotten is that the long-term health of any free-market society is that quality goods and services that fulfill needs should be priced at levels that are reasonable for all involved. Selling or buying at a gross disadvantage ultimately compromises the free-market system and hurts everyone involved.

How do we stem what appears to be a growing tide of violations of good business practices across many industries that we count on in our daily lives? With all the laws and regulations on the books governing business operations, how is it that we continually discover that consumer rights are being violated or fleeced in some way?

If we are successful in getting a meaningful financial reform bill, lawmakers, and regulatory agencies at every level of government will need to proactively enforce policies and operational procedures to close those loopholes that render the public vulnerable to unscrupulous businesses and their penchant for greed. Punishment must fit the crime.

But the public also must stand up and demand diligent enforcement of those laws and regulations if we hope to get rid of what is rotten in the ROI—that almighty, sometimes elusive, driver that many large businesses will stop short of nothing to make.

How can a free market capitalistic society continue to thrive if such practices go unchecked?

Let elected officials, regulatory bureaucrats, and consumers alike, beware.

Published February 26, 2002
The Kansas City Star

Racism and Religion: Southern Baptist Convention Is Doing Something About It

The Southern Baptist Convention, the largest protestant denomination, could elect its first African American president in June. This is a deliberate step to move beyond its long history of promoting and preaching racial segregation, which predates the Civil War. The convention was actually born out of a conflict over slavery. Baptists in the south supported slavery and Baptists in the north refused to appoint missionaries who owned slaves.

But despite the origin of Baptists beliefs and worshipping traditions, Sunday, whether intentional or non-intentional, is arguably the most racially-segregated day of the week in America—irrespective of your denominational affiliation. Whether you attend worship services in a church located in the urban core, a suburban area, or in the valleys and hillsides along winding country roads, it is very likely that the parishioner beside you or across the aisle is of the same race if not the same ethnic group.

Many of us gather in the pews Sunday after Sunday, unbothered and unfettered by the racial homogeneity all around us, even when the edifice and its distinct steeple peers from a neighborhood whose residents may or may not be homogeneous at all. A neighborhood made up of a variety of racial and ethnic groups, members of which have never dared to dawn the church's entrance, or never invited to come in.

Since its convention in 1995, Southern Baptists officially apologized for their history of racism and have been trying to be more inclusive and improve race relations. One can see the transformation occurring in many of the televised services that dominate television screens during week-end services.

But in too many churches in too many communities across the nation, there is no progress at all when it comes to welcoming different races to share in the worship experience.

The Southern Baptist Convention has more than 40,000 churches as members, most of which are in the south and predominantly white. The convention is working hard to expand its base and in recent years, minority churches have seen the greatest growth rate in the convention.

What a great trend. Convention members are the first to acknowledge that they still have a long way to go before true integration occurs across the many congregations. But they are determined to keep moving in the right direction.

Electing Fred Luter, a New Orleans pastor, as its first African American President will be putting the brotherly love that is preached on Sundays into practice.

Many others can take a lesson and perhaps have a new message on Sundays in words and deeds.

Published May 22, 2012
USAonRace.com

Risks of Intergenerational Divide on Democracy

Is the chasm between one generation of Americans and another widening irreparably on several fronts? If so, ultimately, where will it lead?

While we can only speculate about the answers to those questions, there are a few things we can be sure about.

With unprecedented economic growth, unsurpassed technological advances, and major breakthroughs in medicine and health, there is also growing unconcern among and between generations about one of our most sacred institutions—our democratic form of government.

Study results released last week by The Third Millennium, a non-partisan research group, found that the divide between candidates for president and young voters, ages 18-29, has indeed widened. Fewer than one in ten in this age category bothered to vote during the primary elections in most states. In 1972, when eighteen-year-olds were first granted the right to vote, 52 percent voted in the presidential election. In 1996, a mere 24 percent voted.

The report concluded that there is a growing trend of presidential candidates ignoring young voters; and young voters, likewise, ignoring presidential candidates. The report contends that this trend is creating a growing generation of Americans who could care less about elections.

Reasons offered for this intergenerational divide on the political front are ones that we all have heard: a) Candidates ignore young voters because they do not vote anyway; b) Young voters are turned off by unscrupulous politicians.

But perhaps, two of the most disturbing reasons the report offered for this pervasive unconcern among young people were (hold on to your mind) lack of time and lack of interest. Yes.

Of those surveyed, some said they did not have the time to vote, but most said they simply were not interested.

Do not have time? Simply, not interested?

For those of us who are now baby boomers—many of whom were reformers, activists, and certainly engaged— we must wonder what will be the nature and quality of government should we live to become octogenarians and centenarians?

If we fail to stem this growing gulf of disinterestedness, in the long term, where will it leave future generations? America?

It is easy to say the fault lies with suspect politicians and a campaigning process that is often insulting and out of control. We can say such indifference is due to the over emphasis on self-actualization at the expense of community wellbeing. But what are we, the generations that have benefited and continue to benefit from this great democracy, doing to preserve its most sacred tenets within our families?

We have managed to get away from lessons learned, both historical and those that are just common sense. Values and a way of life just do not preserve themselves. They are not self-perpetuating.

The laws, principles, mores, traditions, and values of any society are preserved through deliberate and methodical passage from one generation to another. They are taught in schools, practiced in the daily activities of governmental, economic, religious, and social institutions. In the most ideal sense, the interweaving of these threads that make up the very fabric of a healthy and thriving society should be as much a part of the family dialogue as talking about our next of kin, as searching for our roots—genetic and otherwise. We go through extreme lengths to equip our progeny in the name of longevity and immortality when it comes to family matters. What about society-sustaining matters?

Are we bothering to pass on to our children the importance of what needs to be done to preserve our democratic way of life? If we are not, it begs a number of questions. First, among them: What will it matter if we achieve the most technological advances, find cures for the most dreadful diseases, yet cease to be a civil, caring, and democratic society?

This is the real potential risk if we continue to ignore the intergenerational divide occurring in our political process and fail to do something about the reasons causing it.

Doesn't self-actualization and preserving democratic practices go hand in hand? Ask any immigrant, or those who wish they could immigrate to America.

Published May 2, 2000
The Kansas City Star

Rooting Out Racism Every Day at Every Opportunity

In the fast-paced, information over-load society in which we live, much of what we see and hear remains in our consciousness for a fleeting moment. There is so much that we miss or never see or hear about at all. Out of necessity, we often self-select those areas of interest that obviously impact our immediate situations—today, next week, maybe next year. Too often, to our own detriment, we ignore many other things going on now that will affect our long-term future.

The perennial issues around race, race relations, racism, the oppressed and the oppressors (deliberate or inadvertent), the plight of the disenfranchised across the street, across town, or across the country often get our passing attention, if at all. Rarely, do we bother to ponder, let alone take corrective action, about those situations that are bound to come home to roost someday, one way or the other.

Who would have thought that the "Occupy Wall Street" protest would have spun similar protest in cities all across America—from New York to California, from Washington state to Washington, D.C.? The very media that bombards us with information also instantly connects us. So those protests have gone global. The common theme is that millions of hard-working people are tired of being exploited economically—not getting the same opportunities as the rich and powerful.

Why do we think, or find comfort in the notion, that one day there will not be similar protests from millions of people who have grown tired and worn by the perpetual practices of racial discrimination? Where millions of individuals have grown intolerant of being perceived and treated as a result of some old, inaccurate a derogatory stereotype.

Can we image a time when there might be a rainbow of people, representing many groups, cutting across race and ethnicities finally taking a stand saying, "enough is enough"?

Imagine? We had better.

While they might not make the newspaper headlines or the evening news on local networks or worldwide cable, there are people addressing racist behavior on many fronts. They are occurring every day in many places.

Just this week alone, *Reuters, The New York Times, The Washington Post* reported about a letter sent to Attorney General Eric Holder by the American Civil Liberties Union (ACLU), which objected to the prevalent practice of the FBI conducting investigations of Americans based on their ethnic identities. According to *The Washington Post*, the ACLU claims: "The FBI's own documents con-

firm our worst fears about how it is using its overly expan-
sive surveillance and racial profiling authority…The FBI
has targeted minority American communities around the
country for investigation based not on suspicion of actual
wrongdoing but on the crudest stereotypes about which
groups commit different types of crimes."

The FBI has stated that it understands the position of
the ACLU. But noted that there are legitimate exceptions
where issues of national and border security are concerned.

This issue alone highlights the importance of accurate and
ongoing communications at a minimum; and the importance
of seeking out the real facts about the many different people
that make up America and basing actions on those facts.

How the U.S. government acts is critical to routing out
unwarranted racist behavior.

But there are incidents occurring in communities across
America on a daily basis.

In Hillsboro, Oregon, police officers are calling out the
Ford pickup truck, homes and an elementary school that
were painted with racial slurs hate crimes. Unknown sus-
pects used spray paint to write racial epithets, draw swas-
tikas and leave the KKK (Ku Klux Klan, the most notable
white supremacist group) signature.

Michigan State University administration and board
of trustees have come under fire by students for failing to
respond in a timely fashion to a string of racially charged
incidents on campus. Students are demanding that the
university revisits its diversity and inclusion policies.

In Springfield, Illinois, four universities are teaming with the Coalition to Promote Human Dignity and Diversity to sponsor a series of programs and forums on race relations.

The student group, Students Teaching Against Racism in Society at Ohio State University, has launched a poster campaign to warn Halloween revelers about the insensitivity and ignorance of selecting costumes that depict racial and ethnic stereotypes.

It does not stop there. Even the NBA lockout negotiations are raising questions about its racial and stereotypical overtones. The players, predominantly black, do not know what is good for them; and therefore, the owners, predominantly white, know what is in their (the players) best interest. What is to be made of it?

The point is: race, racism, inaccurate stereotypes still occupy too much space and influence in our daily lives.

What will it take for a real change to come?

Published October 28, 2011
USAonRace.com

Why Can't We All Just Be Americans?

There seems to be certain identifiers attached to some groups of Americans and not others. Why can't we all just be Americans? Have you ever stopped to ponder why not? Could it be simply because of skin color, or how one group looks versus another? It is past time that we stop embracing the systemic, artificial, and inhumane labels that divide us rather than unite us.

One thing is for sure, it certainly cannot be because of where groups immigrated from, or when they did so. America has been made up of immigrant families since the beginning, and still. Native Americans, the Indian tribes that occupied the lands before all of us immigrants came, are the only indigenous people. So why have some labels been consistently used as identifiers to set some immigrant Americans apart?

Some groups and not others are reminded at every opportunity that they are not considered to be just Americans. It happens every time when it comes to filling out papers, getting a job, when it comes to navigating most aspects of American society. It is commonplace to be asked whether you are African American, Asian American, Hispanic American?

Have you ever seen a form of any kind that included boxes to check, which included and required someone to identify as Italian American, Polish American, German American, Jewish American, Irish American, etc., etc., and etc.?

Out of all the immigrants to America, Blacks formed the largest group that was brought here against their will, as slaves, when this country was formed. The ancestry of most American families immigrated here of their own accord, seeking a better life. No matter what their ethnic identity, they have been able to assimilate, to become just Americans. But it is not so for Blacks,

Asians, and Hispanics--and Blacks particularly. Members of all groups work and die for one America.

What is the redeeming value of hanging on to those labels for some groups and not for other groups if not for the sole purposes to maintain social divisions, to deny equal treatment, to deny equal opportunity, and to deny equal access to all that being an American should afford?

It could be argued that Blacks, Asians, and Latinos bear some responsibility for holding onto and perpetuating those labels as they have tried as groups to assimilate or fight for equal rights and opportunities. Some could argue that these groups have tried to hang on to their culture and identity from their homelands. But other groups have, too. They practice and pass down family traditions and cultural practices from their homelands. But they are not confronted with their immigrant identity at every turn, on every form they have to fill out as they live and work in

America.

Have you ever thought about why some Americans are still identified legally as separate when they have been here as long or longer that other groups of Americans? Members of all groups work and die for one America. Not a white America, not a black America, not a yellow or brown America, but for America.

Why can't we all just be Americans? It is a question worthy of serious consideration.

Published April 9, 2021
https://janicesellis.com/blog

Staying Connected Is Getting Tougher

It is true that with all the telecommunication advances, the world is virtually smaller. The vast geographical expanse no longer keeps people visually and telephonically apart. Thanks to the telephone, satellite, and cable television. And do not forget the almighty Internet.

While all the world, those who live in poorer communities and countries, is not connected, there is already a lot of discussion about the need to close the digital divide.

But, in our efforts to close the digital divide, are we widening the personal divide?

Will the ease and convenience of communicating technologically make us more disconnected as neighbors, colleagues, family members—as people?

Admittedly, being able to leave a voice mail message or send an e-mail is a very convenient way to communicate. But wasn't the original intent of these communication tools that they be used when person-to-person communication, either by phone or meeting, was very inconvenient if not impossible? Wasn't their use supposed to be the exception rather than the norm?

So much for intent.

Do not misunderstand the point. Despite the frustration of getting chain-linked voice mail instructions when calling most businesses these days, despite repeatedly getting the voice mail box of business colleagues, and the answering machines of family members and friends, automated communication is better than none at all. But we need to be mindful of its toll, and its contribution to keeping people personally disconnected.

If you think voicemail and e-mail have had its impact on personal interaction among adults, imagine the impact of all the computer and Internet games targeted to three, four and five-year-olds. There are games offering virtual pets, and virtual friends. Kids can stay entertained and connected for hours. While these technological experiences may make kids smarter, will they make them more socially adjusted? More understanding, more caring, better adapted human beings.

There is no substitute for good old-fashioned human interaction.

But with all the technologically advanced communication tools, how does one stay personally connected? Personally, connected to people, to our communities, which are so important to our overall well-being.

How does one assess his or her place, the sense of belonging, in a world where we are both connected and separated by our technological ingenuity?

These may seem like simplistic, or even unimportant, questions on the surface. But the answers play a crucial role in our physical and mental health—the quality of our lives, and in many cases the longevity of our lives.

Recently, I stumbled upon a book by Dr. Edward Hallowel entitled *Connect*. While I have not had an opportunity to finish the book, Dr. Hallowel make a convincing case of how our relationships with others and the communities in which we live play a critical role in our overall well-being.

We know the study results that confirm from childhood to old age, we are healthier both physically and mentally when we feel a strong sense of belonging and it is evident in our daily lives. We know the negative impact of real isolation. No doubt therein lies clues to the potential impact of virtual isolation.

The need to be connected and stay connected with people and causes will become even more important as we move more and more toward a telecommunication society where e-mail, teleconferencing, and of course the phone, are becoming our major avenues to "reach out and touch."

Soon the option to do all of our shopping and visiting (video telephones) electronically will be widely available. Imagine having the option to join a place of worship on the Internet. Religious chat lines are already available.

Perhaps one of the best ways to make technology work for us is to use the time saved to spend more time getting to know people who are important to us. What has happened to the value of walking down the hall to discuss an issue with a colleague? Having a conversation with a neighbor over the backyard fence?

We would do well to remember a few things: No technological convenience can ever replace a hug, a pat on the shoulder, a smile, sharing a meal, engaging in a vigorous debate about something for which you care deeply.

Being virtually connected *is not* the same as the real thing.

Published October 3, 2000
The Kansas City Star

Strengthening Our Families – the Foundation for Our Future

As we come to a close of Black History month, one of the most worthwhile things we can do for our future legacy is to rededicate our efforts to build strong family units.

Sociologists proclaim that many forces bombard the family unit in contemporary society. Many also readily acknowledge that whatever plagues society generally, whether economic problems, educational problems, divorce, single parenting, poor housing, etc., the impact on African American families is much more severe and the ramifications more far-reaching and long-lasting.

In many ways, the black family unit still suffers from the ravages of history. There are many strong black families, headed by one or both parents. There are many others reeling from some indelible scars which originated with the institution of slavery—an institution that did everything in its power to rape and destroy the family unit, separating mother and father, mother, and child. And even though it has been well over a hundred years since that wretched institution supposedly died, the many negative effects are still seen today.

The black family has been imperiled by one destructive force after the other. And the impact can be seen throughout communities across the country. You need only to review a few grim statistics: the vicious cycle of black-on-black crime, higher rates of unemployment during economic prosperity, poor health and limited or no access to the best health care available. By comparison, the black family still, disproportionately, lives in poor housing and blighted neighborhoods. And the feelings of helplessness, complacency, apathy, and general lethargy, is much too high.

Perhaps, the greatest and long-lasting impact of these destructive forces is on the children. They are the ones who find it difficult to have vision, to see beyond their immediate living environment. They are the ones who are more vulnerable, who are likely to succumb to drugs and a life of crime to escape their deprived and disheartening condition. They are the children having children, in part out of ignorance and a lack of direction, in part out of hope and the need to feel important to someone, to show love, to receive love. The result is double jeopardy, double loss. A young girl may never reach her potential; and the child she brings into the world starts out at a disadvantage. For a family unit that is already frail and weak, this can only make it weaker, more vulnerable.

Where do the answers lie? How do we stop the destructive forces? First, we must refuse to believe they are beyond our control. We must commit ourselves to do whatever we can to strengthen the family unit. The answers are neither simple nor easy. Nor can they be achieved overnight. We must tackle, and we are, some very tough problems, like the perpetual dependency on welfare. Welfare is a complicated subject, with complex causes. But relying on welfare breeds more dependency. Welfare is like a pain reliever, temporary and somewhat comforting, but it offers no ultimate cure for what is causing the problem. It is not a job where you can earn enough wages to improve your living conditions. Long term, it often does more harm than good.

As we continue to work for better housing, better education, equal access to jobs and other economic opportunities, we should invest a substantial amount of time with our young people. We must help them overcome many hurdles and misconceptions that can destroy their future—even before they have any idea of what that future can be.

Some basics we need to convey: For starters, to our young men, we must tell them that there is nothing to be proud of or boast about when they father children that they cannot take care of. Our boys need to be told plainly that it does not make them men. And our girls need to be told that becoming pregnant is not proof or guarantee of love from the father who was not ready to be, or the child who could easily grow to be resentful for bringing them into the world under such wretched and stigmatized conditions—conditions, which neither parent is prepared to change.

We must continue to emphasize the absolute need to get an education. Without an education in today's society, the odds of improving your living conditions are firmly stacked against you. We cannot continue to let our children indulge in the rap and "crap" on the radio and ignore the lessons and messages in the classroom.

To achieve appreciation for the value of a strong family unit, and address those needs to build and preserve it, often like any positive outcomes, must be taught, learned, and practiced.

While we cannot undo the past conditions that have left destruction and feelings of hopelessness, we CAN stop them and continue to build a stronger family unit—for future generations.

Let us keep our eyes on the real prize: strengthening our families for the sake of our children.

Published February 22, 2002
The Kansas City Call

Sunday Most Racially Segregated Day

Sunday, whether intentional or non-intentional, is arguably the most racially segregated day of the week in America. Whether you attend worship services in a church located in the urban core, a suburban area, or in the valleys and hillsides along winding country roads, it is very likely that the parishioner beside you or across the aisle is of the same race if not the same ethnic group.

Many of us gather in the pews Sunday after Sunday, unbothered and unfettered by the racial homogeneity all around us, even when the edifice and its distinct steeple peers from a neighborhood whose residents may or may not be homogeneous at all. A neighborhood made up of a variety of racial and ethnic groups, members of which have never dared to dawn the church's entrance, or have never been invited to come in.

The National Congregations Study, which conducted surveys in 1998 and, most recently in 2006—07, confirms that the vast majority of churches throughout the nation are made up of members of the same race or ethnic group.

At first glance, the "Sunday Self-Segregation" phenomenon is easily understandable. After all, our religious beliefs and methods of worship are extensions of our family life, whether Catholic or Protestant, Islamic or Judaic, or some other religion. So, it comes naturally to gather with "our kind." To do otherwise presents a kind of what we instinctively feel is an unwanted and unnecessary dissonance when we find ourselves outside of "our comfort zone."

Such dissonance is often palpable for the visitor who goes to a church predominantly of a different race, as well as for those he or she visits. So, what does that say about our willingness to invite, accept, include others—a brotherly deed that the very religion we embrace teaches and urges us to practice—who on the surface may look and live very unlike us?

Though we may see more diverse congregations in some areas, and certainly on some televised religious services, integrated congregations are far from being the norm.

But in some areas, there is no progress at all when it comes to welcoming different races to share in the worship experience.

There are likely many churches, all over the land, which wish to, and work to remain racially segregated, whether white, black, brown, yellow, or otherwise. Perhaps, even more than we care to fathom.

Do you think we can have true racial integration if we persist in remaining segregated in the worship experience on Sundays, even when we share the same religious beliefs that teach otherwise?

Published January 31, 2015
https://janicesellis.com/blog

Technologies Advance While Human Relations Decline

What does it say about contemporary society when across the globe technologies advance while human relations decline? One would think with the advancement in communication technology, it would be easier for us to connect and stay connected.

Instead, we are plagued with divides. We are divided when it comes to the role of government in our lives, race and gender equality, access to a quality education, trade, and immigration policy, participation in war, on and on.

It should be easy to share factual information and have ongoing conversations to find solutions to the problems and challenges we share in common. This should be especially true when it comes to governmental and political issues. So why isn't good dialogue and communication occurring on the national, regional, state, or local levels of government?

This decline in effective communication among us, the decline in civility, plagues not only the United States, but points across the globe. Technologies advance while human relations decline.

Why?

One could argue there are many reasons: a lack of understanding of the gravity of issues; self-interest being put above the public good; and the growing misuse of technology by passing false information as truth.

But, perhaps, the greatest reason of all is the absence of a collective will to stand up, speak out, about things that we witness or experience that are clearly wrong or not good to make our society better. We readily tolerate speech and actions that are or will be detrimental to families, communities, and our country—even the well-being of the planet.

We find ourselves in awe and applauding as technologies advance while human relations decline. It is not just in the political arena. Often, it is evident in the family and work environment. We have all the communication technology at our fingertips and yet we fail to communicate with each other. Sadly, we seem to be fine with it.

Technological advancements in other areas like medicine, transportation, agriculture, space exploration, environmental preservation, etc. abound. But ultimately, what good is it if it is not used to improve the human condition?

As long as we stand by and allow greed, biases, prejudices, and other forms of self-interest to prevail, we will continue to see technologies advance while human relations decline.

How unfortunate. How potentially tragic. But it is not too late to stand up and do our part.

Published June 16, 2019
https://janicesellis.com/blog

Indiscriminate Use of Racial Stereotypes Is Too Costly for All

Whether it is our thoughts about black teens wearing hoodies or baggie pants, or white kids wearing punk hairstyles and mystic tattoos; whether it is rich kids driving BMWs and Corvettes to high schools; or Hispanics kids driving decorated low-riders. We all have and use stereotypes that wield a lot of persuasive power, intentionally or unintentionally in our daily lives.

The influence they have on our perceptions and actions toward each other too often is not very good and does little to improve our understanding of and relations with one another.

The costs, limitations and hurtfulness abound.

We do not have to wait to have a dialogue about the harmful effects of stereotypes when we allow them to blindly govern our thought about and behavior toward others who do not share our skin color, do not live in our neighborhood, who like different kinds of foods or who prefer and wear different kinds of clothes.

We have become too accustomed to relying on attitudes and labels, rightly or wrongly, passed from one generation to the next, without ever taking time to examine them or bother to learn firsthand whether such labels and stereotypes are true, bare any semblance to reality. Yet we allow these notions and presuppositions to govern our lives—often irrespective of the settings.

We do not see stereotypes just playing out in the law enforcement and criminal justice arenas, but we see it playing out in how kids of color are taught or not taught in schools. We see in play out in whether and how people of color are hired and/or promoted, or not promoted, in the workplace. We see stereotypes at play when people of color go to buy a house, get equitable and market rate mortgages even when they are well-educated with good jobs making them very creditworthy.

Labels and stereotypes—what power they wield, more often negatively defining and destructive than not.

Most of us are often not in tune, sometime totally oblivious, to how other labels—sociological, economic, political, racial, religious—affect how we go about our business on a day-to-day basis. Assigning and using labels within itself is not the problem. This phenomenon is perfectly normal according to sociologists. Labels, symbols, rituals, like laws and rules, provide order to our society. Such practices determine the nature and quality of any civilization. The lack of norms causes the collapse of a civilization. So, labels and symbols, in and of themselves, are not bad.

How labels are used becomes the problem—when they evolve into negative stereotypes. Rightly or wrongly, we place people and things in "boxes" or categories to manage and guide our conduct toward them and determine many other decisions we make.

Many minority groups (and minority is a label) could testify about the impact labels have had on their ability, or lack thereof, to fully assimilate in society and enjoy the opportunities and privileges afforded "non-minorities." The minority label is not just confined to racial or ethnic groups. Minorities can also pertain to beliefs, religious affiliations, political identity, i.e., conservative vs. liberal vs. independent, socio-economic status, etc.

Categorical and stereotypical labels can be harmful—very harmful. While they often provide a level of comfort and ease as one interacts in his/her environment, they often serve as blinders to the discovery of truth and determining reality.

Will you continue to allow labels and stereotypes that have been passed on by family members or perpetuated in mainstream media to determine how you think or act?

Or will you bother to examine and verify? While you owe others the benefit of having an opened mind as you encounter them, more importantly, you owe it to yourself.

The indiscriminate use of a stereotype is costly not only to the person it is being used against, but also to the one who is using it.

Published April 6, 2012
USAonRace.com

The Power of Words to Effect Change

The power of words to bring about change is an effective tool to improve the quality of our lives when used wisely. How do you see the state or quality of life within your immediate family, your neighborhood, community or city, your state, our nation? Do we see ourselves as islands or do we believe we all are interconnected to a lesser or greater degree?

Do we ever pause to ponder such questions amid the hustle and bustle and daily demands of family and work? Sadly, it is likely that most of us are so hurried and busy living that we do not pause to give a fleeting thought to the times of our lives, let along use the power of words to bring about change. Instead, we often go along to get along.

Whether it is the state of the economy, the quality of education available, increased gun violence in our homes and on our city streets, or surprise terrorist attacks where we work, worship, or venues where we gather with friends and family—they are all issues that can be addressed using the power of words in meaningful dialogue.

We must take time to read, listen, think, analyze, and come together to act upon these issues and events, examining the potentially lasting impact on our lives, the lives of our children, our grandchildren, and their children. It all can be achieved with the power of words.

We have all heard the sayings, "If you don't know where you have been, how can you know where you are going?" We must look at today's events, from yesterday's and tomorrow's perspective, and the more we observe, the more we will realize that broad and sweeping changes and conditions develop over time. Many are unnoticed until it is too late because we are not engaged.

Decisions and policies, many of which are far-reaching and life-altering, are often talked about and acted upon long before we see the nature and kind of fruit they will bear—good or bad. More importantly, the lasting impact on the quality of our lives.

The fate of a society is much like raising children. What a child ultimately becomes is as a result of the kind of nurturing and experiences he or she encounters over time. That is not to ignore that natural events beyond anyone's control can also have lasting impact. But such events will never excuse or justify our apathy, our silence, and our inaction.

Each of us needs to take time to find a quiet place on a frequent basis (at the end of a day, sitting or driving on a Sunday afternoon) and ponder the long-term implications of what is going on around us.

There are examples everywhere, in our communities, our cities, the nation, and on the world stage, where people use the power of words. History is loaded with examples of both heroes and ordinary people who cared enough to speak up and speak out. They understood the meaning of powerful voices.

The power of words is always available to us. Many have used the power of words to impact and improve the human condition and they knew that meaningful and lasting change would not come over night.

Now is a good time to ask what has changed significantly (for better or worse) over the last 10 years? 20 years? 30, 40, 50 years? How did those changes come about? Was it because of the power of words or was it because someone took advantage of our silence?

The real and overriding question is: What conditions are we willing to just accept, when the power of words could be used to bring about positive and meaningful change?

More importantly, are we willing to speak up and speak out?

Published March 12, 2016
https://janicesellis.com/blog

The Times Beg for a New Conversation: Will Civility and the Common Good Reign Again?

As the end of another year approaches, as we prepare to celebrate yet another Holiday Season when we harkened back to old family traditions, taking time to prepare old homemade meals, get reacquainted and bask in the comfort of family and friends, we will unlikely be able to totally escape the sense of unease and disconnectedness we feel about the times we live in the United States and the world.

A real sense of unease and disconnectedness pervade our psyche about the global civilized world we thought was emerging in its fullest sense, as we embraced the dawn of the 21st century just more than a decade ago, to one that seems today rifted with cultural, religious, and economic chasms so wide that they appear to be permanent divides.

Where has the pre-eminent tenet, of always working to achieve the greatest good for the greatest number, and the notion that civility should rule the day, gone?

The forces, evil and otherwise, that brought us to this point in human civilization have been brewing for a long,

long time. And unfortunately, many of us still may not have gotten the messages.

During the last decade, we have been attacked on our own soil. We seem to be in the grips of an economic downturn with no immediate relief in sight. We have been subjected to pillage and rape by corporate greed and phantom investment practices that have gone unchecked. We have managed to send representatives, of the people to Washington, who have been unable to get the people's agenda done because of personal agendas of their own.

Where has fighting for the common good and practicing civility gone?

It is little wonder that we long for the way things used to be. We wish we could go on with our lives, working to fulfill our dreams and making the world better than we found it just as we always have in the sovereign American way.

But could it be, that amid all the political impasse, economic uncertainty, and compromised sense of safety, there is greater opportunity to reconnect with some fundamental and inescapable tenets of a healthy society that we may have lost sight of?

It really boils down to some serious reflections. Each of us needs to rid ourselves of those thoughts and habits that may not foster positive societal outcomes and replace them with ones that bear repeating:

- The fact is no individual, race, or country is the center of the universe. We all have a place. We all have purpose and roles to play. Why can we not find more mutual respect and more common ground to address shared challenges and problems that could advance all society?

- The sustained quality of one's life need not be based on the exploitation of other human beings. The exploited eventually seek revenge or change. History is replete with examples and the Occupy Movement, occurring all across America and in many places across the globe, is just another.
- Wanton selfishness is not a virtue. There are only short-term gains, if any when one goes about his or her daily affairs with utter disregard for their neighbor, colleague, friend, relative, or a stranger.
- Choosing ignorance over knowledge is never wise. Ignorance generally is the breeding ground for vulnerability and existing in a state of perpetual and at a costly disadvantage.
- Turning a blind eye or living in denial solves nothing.

As we come to the close of another year, celebrate another holiday season, perhaps it should be more that tradition as usual. Tradition as usual may have allowed us to become complacent and accepting of human degradation and atrocities right here on American soil and abroad.

We must become and remain vigilant, and come together to fight the many ugly forces—religious fanaticism, ethnic cleansing, racial discrimination, and economic exploitation—that reign in our immediate and distant world.

Racial and religious intolerance have always been with us. They play a central role in the annals of history of too many countries. What common ties of human nature that bind us. No one owns bragging rights when it comes to always doing what is best for all of humanity.

Understanding that being different does not automatically mean better or worse, it simply means different. How you view being different can be enlightening or enslaving. How much longer can we afford to refuse to see, acknowledge and try to understand the different among us, rather than shun, alienate, exploit or destroy them?

The misuse of money, power, and ingenuity has often made it easy for us to ignore an age-old premise: We are in this journey of life together. Our mutual regard will move us forward or prevent us from becoming the best we can be. Perhaps we have omitted these realizations in our conversations.

When we look around us, in our homes, in our religious, educational, and political institutions, discussing the need to return to civility toward each other should be as much a part of any dialogue or discussion as the subject at hand.

If not, how can we expect things to get better?

Published November 21, 2011
USAonRace.com

To Wear a Mask or Not Wear a Mask

To wear a mask, or not wear a mask, is only one aspect of the challenge we have as a nation to stop the spread of coronavirus. Yet, it seems to have become a major issue for the wrong reasons. Some see the issue as a political one, showing allegiance to one party or the other. Others see it as an infringement on their individual rights and freedom.

Did anyone ever imagine that a face covering could cause such a stir? There was a time when the meaning of wearing a face covering was pretty clear. Crooks often wore them, and still do, to commit a crime. That was the most common negative meaning. Doctors, nurses, and others in the medical profession have worn, and still wear, masks routinely to protect the patient and themselves. So, why has to wear a mask or not wear a mask become such a vitriolic and divisive question? To the point where people are protesting, getting into brawls, brandishing weapons.

When coronavirus first begin to surge in the United States, the main issue was there were not enough masks, particularly professional grade masks, for the doctors and nurses and other first responders caring for those falling ill. There was a shortage of other protective wear. In many states, now that there is a resurgence of the virus, there seems to be another shortage of masks and protective wear for health care providers. Yet the general public is caught in the morass of to wear a mask or not wear a mask. A simple mask.

Why as thousands of our fellow Americans continue to fall ill and die of the virus on a daily basis wouldn't those of us who have been fortunate enough not to become sick do everything in our power to protect ourselves, our family, our neighbors, or anyone we come in contact with?

According to the infectious disease experts, doctors, nurses, and others dealing with this deadly virus, wearing masks will be highly effective in getting this virus under control. Wearing a mask is not a political statement. Wearing a mask is not an infringement on anyone's individual rights. Do we have a cure or even an effective treatment protocol for this virus?

To wear a mask or not wear a mask could really be a question of whether you are willing to fall ill, make someone ill, and worse yet, die or be disabled in some way for the rest of your life.

Given the circumstances, to wear a mask is the least that we as Americans can do for ourselves, our family, our neighbors, the overworked doctors and nurses, shuttered businesses, and the health and economic well-being of America.

To wear a mask or not wear a mask? Please consider the consequences of your answer to that question.

Published July 22, 2020
https://janicesellis.com/blog

Use and Misuse of Labels

Labels wield a lot of persuasive power—intentionally or unintentionally.

I am not speaking of labels on the commodities (clothes, foods, etc.) we buy. Although in our efforts to be informed consumers, we read and rely on the representation of those labels too. The concern here is about the influence of labels on a broader scale.

Labels, like symbols, rituals, laws, and rules, provide a kind of order. Such ordering of things is a necessary part of any civilized society. This phenomenon is perfectly normal according to sociologists. So, labels, in and of themselves, are not bad.

But how labels are used can often be a problem whether the label is applied to a group or an individual. Rightly or wrongly, we place people and things in "boxes" or categories to manage and guide our conduct toward them, and to determine many other decisions we make.

Categorical and stereotypical labels can be harmful—very harmful. While they often provide a level of comfort and ease as one interacts in his/her environment, they also serve as blinders to the discovery of truth and determining reality. We become comfortable accepting our fictitious creations and occasional truths as prevailing and impenetrable facts.

Perhaps the use and misuse of labels is no more evident than during our national elections. Politicians take comfort in assigning labels to different groups to predict their voting behavior. Labels are assigned to the young, the old, baby boomers, and minorities.

But let the labelers beware.

Results of a comprehensive poll of likely Hispanic voters conducted by Knight Ridder Newspapers, and reported in Sunday's *Kansas City Star*, may go a long way in making us pause before we unilaterally categorize a race or ethnic group and act blindly on those categorizations.

The poll results show, apparently to the surprise of some, that among Hispanics, you will find their views about government and issues to be very similar to those of "mainstream" America. While 60 percent of Hispanics polled consider themselves Democrats, a great majority of Hispanics describes themselves as politically conservative which makes them a prime target for Republican candidates.

The headline in the *Kansas City Star's* article describes Hispanics as "politically diverse." Could this be a new label? Will it have the same sticking power as the label, "liberal Democrats," has had on African Americans?

The article in the *Kansas City Star* acknowledged

that the attention paid to Hispanics is not surprising since, according to the Census Bureau, they make up 11 percent of the U.S. population and are expected to surpass African Americans as the nation's largest minority group within five years.

Perhaps another reason the attention is shifting to Hispanics is the broad-sweeping negative impacts the label, "blacks do not vote," has had on African Americans as a group. The perception is based, unfortunately, on the consistent low-voter turnout in most local and national elections. Many candidates disregard issues and concerns of African Americans because of that very label. Republican candidates often ignore African American voters because of that label and the belief that if African Americans bother to vote they will vote overwhelmingly for democratic candidates.

Consequently, what could be strong political leverage by the nation's current largest minority group is significantly minimized because both candidates and African American voters refuse to take steps to change these limiting, even crippling, labels.

Too often, as we go about our business on a daily basis, we are not always aware how labels—sociological, economic, political, racial, religious—affect our wellbeing, positively and negatively.

What labels have been assigned to you, your race, ethnic or religious group? Are they accurate or inaccurate? If labels aren't working for you, and having a positive impact, should not steps be taken to change them? To ignore harmful labels is foolhardy.

Published July 25, 2000
The Kansas City Star

Common Sense During Coronavirus Crisis

Relying upon and using common sense during coronavirus crisis could be the safest path as we continue to receive contradictory messages from national, state, and local leadership. No matter where you live, you are likely not getting complete facts or clear direction on how to keep you and your family safe.

The fact that there is not a national plan or guidelines for how or when communities, businesses, or schools should resume normal activities pose a grave risk. Leaving it up to each entity to determine and decide operational and social distancing rules and guidelines is bound to bring about mixed outcomes. No community or business is an island. This is where using common sense during coronavirus crisis must come in.

Furthermore, how will the various rules and guidelines to ensure safety and minimum spread of the virus be enforced in the various public venues? In restaurants, shopping malls, barbershops, beauty salons, and all manner of other businesses? Schools—from daycare centers to colleges?

Will or can protective masks, gloves consistently be worn by everyone? Will or can minimum social distancing of remaining six feet apart be practiced and maintained by everyone? Just look around and you will readily see the answers for yourself.

To further complicate what you should or should not be doing, new information is being put out there almost daily. Using common sense during coronavirus crisis might be the best method to keep you and your loved ones safe.

For example, we recently learned that remaining six feet apart may not be good enough since a vigorous cough, even talking loudly, by an infected person good project the viral germs far beyond six feet. We are learning that children who may have had the virus weeks before are showing life-threatening conditions weeks later. So, what should be the guidelines for opening businesses, schools?

The mixed messages around testing, the availability of tests and who can get them is dizzying. Whether there are effective treatment methods, using existing drug therapies, is very confusing. And the likely availability of a safe and effective vaccine depends on who you listen to, selfish and ambitious politicians, or trained and experienced scientists.

Using common sense during coronavirus crisis will likely be your best defense in the short term until scientists and leaders come together to determine what is needed to either eradicate the virus or manage it successful in the coming months or years—however long it might take.

Published May 15, 2020
https://janicesellis.com/blog

What Is Your Dream?

What is your dream beyond your personal desires? What causes prick your heart and soul deeply enough to spend time to change them, make things better for the disenfranchised among us?

Martin Luther King, Jr. had a dream. He followed it. He spent his life, and lost it, trying to turn his dream into reality.

After the celebration and the commemoration of his life, let us put into practice, like him, much of what he preached. Let each of us carve out a cause or causes and continue to work for a quality life for the disenfranchised who live within our community, our city, our nation.

Most people remember the famous "I Have a Dream" speech which King delivered during the march on Washington, D.C. in 1963. But the fire that burned within King's soul, that led him to dedicate his life toward eradicating social evil and injustice, started long before—nearly 20 years earlier when he traveled to Dublin, Georgia as a senior in high school to deliver "The Negro and the Constitution" in an oratory contest.

Perhaps, it was just a flicker then. But as you follow King's life through college and the seminary, you see that flicker grow into a flame. The more he saw and heard, the more he could not turn a blind eye or a deaf ear. He set out on a life-long journey to eradicate human injustice.

Yet, more than five decades later after the march on Washington and after some progress and much sacrifice by many people, we find ourselves at critical crossroads where we can choose to go backwards, standstill, or move forward.

In recent years, one could argue that we have lost ground. Schools across America are still segregated, some more than ever. Voting rights continue to be challenged in many states, making it more difficult for blacks and other minorities to exercise their right to vote.

There is still discrimination occurring in the job market, access to housing, and access to higher education whether it involves admission to colleges, universities of technical vocational institutions.

Discrimination is still rampant in the justice system when it comes to racial profiling, traffic stops, or issuing the same punishments for the same crime. There are injustices even among how schools' discipline black children and white children for the same misconduct.

What are we willing to do to confront the racial inequality and injustices still prevalent in many aspects of life all across America?

Doing something, continuing to root out inequality and injustice where we encounter it, is the greatest tribute we can pay to Martin Luther King, Jr., and others like him.

When King took up the fight to rid this country of racial discrimination, he knew he was not dealing with a condition that came about in a short period of time. He also knew that change would not come over night.

The real question is: Will we continue to let such conditions define the times of our lives?

What is your dream to make humanity better?

Published January 19, 2015
USAonRace.com

Where Are the Leaders Like Gandhi, Mother Teresa, Mandela, King?

With all the poverty, abusive power, oppression, rampant racial hatred, and discrimination in the United States and across the world, where are the strong and committed leaders? Where are the men and women who are willing to fight the gallant fight to continue to improve the plight of humanity?

Where are the leaders like Gandhi, Mother Teresa, Mandela, King?

With the resurgence of racial hatred and the growing deterioration of race relations in this country, it seems that all the progress made by King and the Civil Rights Movement is now on a slippery slope. Perhaps that bane of evil, racial hatred, has really never been that far away—just waiting for the right conditions to raise its ugly head.

Those conditions seem to be spreading in recent years, creating a dangerous and combustible atmosphere. How else can the recent burning of the three historic black churches in Louisiana by a 21-year-old white supremacist be explained? Church burnings in 2019. That was common in 1940s, 1950s, and the 1960s during the height of the Civil Rights Movement.

Why are some officers, in police departments all across the country, comfortable using excessive force against Black people, many of whom are unarmed or not guilty of committing any crime? Why are the urban areas, which are predominantly black, continually plagued by sub-standard housing, poor schools, high unemployment, high crime, and persistent higher rates of poverty?

But these conditions are not just in the United States. They exist in many parts of the world, especially in under-developed countries and those ruled by dictators and tyrants. The work that Mahatma Gandhi, Mother Teresa, and Nelson Mandela spent their lives doing is still sorely needed.

Where are the leaders like Gandhi, Mother Teresa, Mandela, King? We need unflappable leaders who are will-ing to resume such humanitarian work. What a shame it will be to allow their work and the progress, to improve the plight of their fellow citizens, be undone. But that seems to be the path we are on.

We need ongoing strong positive voices to fight against, deter, and drown out the growing racial hatred, the abuse, brutality, and oppressive acts that go along with it.

Published April 4, 2019
https://janicesellis.com/blog

White Folks and Black Folks

White folks and black folks, alike, have some deep-seated and unflattering views about each other. Many are pervasive and sadly too often make us comfortable going about our daily lives disrespecting, judging, and avoiding any meaningful association.

Here are some common views that control our thoughts and perceptions about each other, even though we may not readily express them.

White folks wonder why some black teenagers would rather sell drugs, shoot a fellow teenager for money or a jacket and rob the elderly. Black folks wonder why some white teenagers from wealthy and not-so wealthy neighborhoods choose to build bombs and go on shooting rampages and kill fellow classmates, teachers, and family members.

White folks think there are more able-bodied black folks getting a free ride on the welfare rolls than there are whites. Black folks wonder why any able-bodied white person needs to be on welfare when they have an easier time getting gainfully employed than their black counterparts.

Black folks think affirmative action and set asides are needed to level the playing field. White folks think such measures are reversed discrimination.

There are also those black and white folks who think none of the above. They understand that we all are the sum total of our experience, and that begins and is shaped by the family unit of which we are a part, along with the social, cultural, and economic circumstances that play a role.

There are Blacks and whites that have immovable faith in the human will and spirit to overcome adversity and impoverished conditions. They fervently believe that someday race will not define how we see each other, or how well we work to build stronger families for a better America through better education, gainful employment, quality housing, good neighborhoods, and other supportive services.

There are black folks and white folks who recognize that the family unit holds the key. It must be strong. It must be healthy.

Irrespective of the situations we as people find ourselves—some we share as black and white families, others we do not—they did not come about overnight. Our children, and their actions good or bad, represent the culmination of values, beliefs, practices, and conditions passed from one generation to another.

The American family unit—black or white—in all its forms is at a precarious time in its history. While some have been blessed with privilege, and others plagued and imperiled by paucity, promoting the health and well-being of all families, ultimately, holds the cure.

We must get beyond the negative stereotypes prevalent among many of us and begin to focus on the good that defines the majority of black folks and white folks.

Published March 6, 2015
https://janicesellis.com/blog

Race And Interracial Issues: Why Do They Make Us Squirm

There are many of us who would like to believe that race and interracial issues are no longer a major problem in this county. But if we just look around us, we will witness incidents almost on a daily basis that whisper or scream to us that bigotry, prejudice, and racism are not just alive and well, but thriving.

What painful reminders that old habits, old ways of thinking, separatist traditions linger, die a slow death, if indeed they taste death at all.

The Associated Press' reportage of a white Louisiana justice of the peace officer's recent denial of a marriage license to an interracial couple is just one small example of the racist and separatist practices that undoubtedly occur every single day in this great country whose very existence came about and still depend upon people of every shade and hue.

So, Keith Bardwell, the justice of the peace officer, who refused to marry interracial couples, has taken it upon himself, and believes himself, to be the preserver or racial purity for the sake and well-being of any unborn children and those white and Blacks who do not readily accept them.

What piety. Mr. Bardwell the great purveyor, single-handedly determining what is in the best interest of posterity, the community, and society in his neck of the woods.

The real question is: Who is going to save that community and the greater society from the likes of Keith Bardwell?

The future well-being of our children, our communities, our cities, our nation, our society will continue to be at risk until we become comfortable with having an honest, open, and ongoing conversation—as uncomfortable, painful, as they might be—about those matters of race that have plagued us historically and continue to do so.

The vestiges of racism in this country have far-reaching influence on the negative forces that we confront daily, and they severely compromise the short-term and long-term impact of precious resources at our disposal.

Continuing to believe that separate but equal has real value and weight in a world that becomes more intra-interconnected and intra-inter dependent by the minute is sheer folly. Such a belief gives not only a false sense of security, but a dangerous one.

Hanging on to such anachronistic ideas is only a breeding ground for extremists and terrorists, whether they come in white hooded robes, serpentine turbans or shrouds, or AK-47 toting mercenaries.

America is not the only country with race relations challenges. Like global warming, it is an issue that continues to threaten the planet in lesser or worse degrees. At worst, we have our vigilante and white supremist groups while other countries have their ethnic cleansing. And like global warming, if we continue to ignore race relations, it could ultimately be our undoing.

With global warming and all the other issues we face here at home and across the globe, why do we need to continually spend precious energy, time, and resources trying to highlight and hold on to those superfluous, insignificant things that divide us like, skin color, the food we eat, the music we listen to, where we gather to worship even if we believe in the same God but call Him by a different name?

At what point, will we spend time and energy to better understand our differences, take time to celebrate what we hold in common and what binds us as human beings. We are all a part of one race: The human race. Until we accept that fact as one which sets us apart from everything else on planet earth, then we will never make progress on those daily issues that divide us or the real issues that threaten our very existence.

Silence, denial, and fear are the real enemies in tackling those issues and matters around race that we face. What a shame because it need not be if we could just let go of those false comfort zones of separateness, and notions of superiority.

Published October 16, 2009
https://janicesellis.com/blog

Why Is Donald Trump So Appealing?

Why is Donald Trump so appealing to many Americans, young, middle age, and seniors alike? The answer is neither very simply nor very obvious. It is not just about the state of politics or the economy in the United States today. By most standards, the economy has improved significantly during the last seven years under the Obama administration.

The state of politics? Well, that is a different issue. Yes, many citizens are sick and tired of the stalemate in Washington between President Obama and the Republican dominated Congress. Yes, citizens are tired of the vitriol, racist and obstructionist rhetoric spewing from the mouths of Republican Senators and Congressmen.

Why is Donald Trump so appealing? No doubt this seven-year atmosphere has contaminated the political soil and has turned out to be fertile breeding ground for a Donald Trump to rise.

Yes, there is this spoken and unspoken notion that with the growing presence of minorities of all colors and origins, white America need to take their country back. There is growing fear from the Census Bureau's prediction that within the next twenty to thirty years, the United States will be a nation of minorities. No one group, white, black, or Hispanic, will be in the majority.

There will be a more even distribution of political power if not economic power. This means that those who have dominated this country for more than two hundred years, exercised power and held all other groups at bay, have growing fear and concerns—justifiable or not.

Why is Donald Trump so appealing?

Those are the more obvious reasons. What is less obvious and what we often forget about are the reasons and profiles of those who founded America. Many who immigrated to the new world had grown tired and weary of the government and King of England.

We all recall the rebellion against "taxation without representation," the lack of religious freedom—essentially the absence of many tenets of our Bill of Rights, which comprise the foundation, the very backbone of this country.

But England also took this rebellion as an opportunity to get rid of its dissidents, its rejects. The Statue of Liberty's inscription is legendary: "Give me your tired, your poor, your huddled masses yearning to breathe free, the wretched refuse of your teeming shore. Send these, the homeless, tempest-tossed to me, I lift my lamp beside the golden door!"

Do these words ring true, back then and now, irrespective of the color of your skin? Has that creed been equally applied?

Now, you think about the many reasons why Donald Trump has so much appeal.

Why is Donald Trump so appealing? It is a question worth pondering, looking beneath the surface.

Published March 21, 2016
https://janicesellis.com/blog

Misleading the Public Is Very
Dangerous and Destructive

Why is it that so many of our trusted leaders do not realize that misleading the public is very dangerous and destructive? When you hear the constant barrage of false and misleading information, it leaves you scratching your head wondering what good do perpetrators expect to get out of it. One can easily conclude that it must be for some selfish agenda, some selfish gain.

But at what costs? Just look at the negative consequences that have occurred across our nation as a result of supposedly caring leaders constantly pushing exaggerated, one-sided, distorted, and downright false information to a vulnerable public. Sadly, they take advantage of a public that is relying on those in charge to tell the truth, to lead the way, to advise on what should be supported as well as what should not be supported.

Misleading the public is very dangerous and destructive. And at what costs? The greatest example that we have seen this play out is with the Covid pandemic that still rages. Had the public been told factual and accurate information as leaders became aware of it, the outcomes when it comes to the scale of infections, deaths, loss of jobs and a devastated economy could have been minimized. False information about wearing masks and taking vaccines remains a challenge. Many elected officials and leaders bear responsibility.

Then, of course, there are the ongoing misleading and false information being kept alive about the 2020 Presidential election. How the election was stolen, how fraudulent voting was rampant. If fact, no evidence has been presented to substantiate these claims. Yet, hundreds of pieces of legislation are being introduced, whether warranted or not, to make voting more difficult for legal citizen instead of making it more convenient. Who, at the end of the day will pay for this? Misleading the public is very dangerous and destructive, which ends up being very costly in so many ways.

So, what are we, a trusting public, to do? Many major issues we face as a country, as a society, can be traced back to the proliferation of information that has been distorted, incomplete, and manipulated for reasons other than what is in the public's best interest. Whether it is increased violence, racial unrest, distrust in government, etc. Sit a while, pick one issue, and think about what you believe, and why. What is the source(s) of your information and knowledge?

Misleading the public is very dangerous and destructive. What can we do about it? It is up to each of us to take responsibility to always seek the truth. We can start by always examining what we hear, what we see, what we read. We cannot be gullible consumers.

The saying, "information is power" is no longer true in the climate of misinformation that we live in today. It must be replaced by "Accurate information is power." Accurate information should rule the day and guide our decisions and actions.

Published April 2, 2021
https://janicesellis.com/blog

When Appearance Matters More Than Reality

In fighting the coronavirus, who and what do we put at risk and sacrifice when appearance matters more than reality and truth? Do you care about how things look more than what is really going on when it comes to the health and well-being of you and your family? Do you really care about your leaders looking and sounding tough, when you are losing your job, when businesses are closing and suffering is all around you?

Whether we care to consider or to admit it or not, it begs the question: What price have we as a nation paid because more emphasis has been placed on creating false appearances? During the last months as the nation has confronted the coronavirus pandemic, we have seen how much pain, damage, illness, death, job loss, business closures, and other bad consequences that have occurred and continue to occur when appearance matters more than reality and truth.

It is one thing to care about appearances. It is quite another to create false appearances. In fact, when appearance matters more than reality, when situations are not portrayed factually and accurately, the consequences can be not only detrimental but downright dangerous. Nowhere has this played out in catastrophic proportions that with the handling of the coronavirus.

Covid-19 has always been a dangerous and deadly virus. But national leadership in the United States has failed to implement a coordinated fight against it, to minimize the number of infections and deaths, job losses and business closures. The leadership of this nation, from the President to Senators, appointed cabinet officials and other Trump supporters have placed more importance on promoting misrepresentation and ill-conceived facts.

When the impression is created that the virus is not deadly and dangerous, who does it benefit? More importantly, how many people are harmed and put at risk when appearance matters more than reality, especially from the leadership that you trust to tell you the truth?

Within the last six months, more than two hundred thousand Americans have lost their lives. More than seven million Americans are infected, with tens of thousands becoming infected daily. Tens of millions of Americans have lost their jobs. Millions of businesses have had to shutter their doors. Millions and millions of American cannot see their loved ones, whether free of or infected with the virus.

Many of those who have adhered to and promoted false appearances have now fallen victim themselves. This includes President Trump, Senators, and many of those around him who support the false appearance that Covid-

19 is not a dangerous and deadly virus that is not yet under control.

Perhaps worst of all, when appearance matters more than reality, there is a tremendous erosion of trust, which could have long-term consequences once truth has been revealed. Based upon what you see and experience versus what you hear, what do you believe?

Published October 5, 2020
https://janicesellis.com/blog

We Can Have Shared Values Amid our Differences

Americans seem to be at odds about nearly everything. Too often, we seem to forget that we can have shared values amid our differences. Can you identify national values that unite us as Americans?

If so, take a moment and jot them down, or discuss them with someone. What would you put on a blank page?

If not, where do you think those values have gone that once united us? Those that gave us a common sense of purpose despite those social, economic, and political areas that still need improvement? We can have shared values amid our differences.

We seem to have forgotten that unity in purpose can be achieved amid differences and imperfections. It occurs in many aspects of our daily lives—in family, at work, in organizations and clubs, even in church or religious identity.

America has faced some critical divisive moments that threatened its very future, most notable the Civil War. Where do you think we are as a nation?

Do you think we have shared values amid our differences?

Some would argue that the disunity that is so visible today has always been there, existing just beneath a façade of one America. That the United States of America has never been a country of states that shared binding values and principles, perhaps except when we were at war, and not always then.

Today, more and more, it seems we have only been united superficially, symbolically. Deep down, one must ask does the majority of Americans believe in values that foster a common humanity afforded all citizens regardless of race, religion, economic status, gender, or age.

Who and what America stands for is coming more into question at home and abroad.

More so than ever, America looks like a nation that is losing its identity and is struggling to define its core values and a path forward.

We can have shared values amid our differences.

It is left up to us as Americans to uphold and live those values that will change the course of disunity that we are currently on.

But do we even know, anymore, what those values are, which most Americans could agree upon today, that will bind us together as a nation?

Published September 24, 2021
https://janicesellis.com/blog

Values and Laws that Make America Great

The values and laws that make America great are at risk for being replace by ones that are less noble, less honorable, and less workable. Where are the defenders of the Constitution and its Amendments that have set this nation apart from any other? What has happened to respect for and adherence to the rule of law? What has happened to freedom of the press? For starters. This erosion, like cancer, is spreading.

Fundamentally, it seems our representative government, which should be *of* the people and *by* the people is losing its way. The voices and defenders of truth and honesty, when it comes to public discourse and advancing public policy, seem to be drowning in a sea of lies and distortions. The lies and distortions are coming from those who hold the most visible and powerful positions in this nation: The President, some Senators, and some Representatives.

Are we really becoming a country, a citizenry that finds acceptable the blatant disregard for honesty, truth, and the rule of law? Is such behavior the new normal? The values and laws that make America great are being ignored and turned upside down. To whom do we turn?

America, the beautiful. Is it now only a song, with empty words? No doubt, many of us long to hold on to what makes America beautiful. No doubt, many of us long for conduct and decorum from our leaders that will honor America and its citizens. No doubt, we long for a President, Vice President, Senators, and Representatives who are great role models.

There was a time when aspiring to be a public servant, an elected official, was an honorable and noteworthy profession. Who can you point to as great role models for your children, your grandchildren, for yourself? Who do you look up to as a model public official, who works for the best interest of the people who elected him/her, who works for the best interest of America?

What we are witnessing today from the highest offices in our land is not just shameful, hurtful, it is putting the very values and laws that make America great at risk.

The future of America and how it will be governed is at a critical crossroads. We, the people, can only determine which road will be taken.

Published September 27, 2019
https://janicesellis.com/blog

Part Two

Commemorations

Our core values and sense of ethics are manifested in what historical events, traditions, and public persons we celebrate and commemorate with holidays, monuments, statues, and other recognitions. This also applies to family, school, religious and community celebrations and commemorations. That is the focus of this collection of commentaries.

Prelude: Meaningful Ways to Celebrate America's Bicentennial

America will soon have an occasion to celebrate.

The Bicentennial should be a time for America to take inventory to see if it is living out the true intentions of its creed.

What were the intentions of our founding fathers when they set out to give America a new and separate identity from England, the motherland? Have we grown ideologically, or have we abandoned our ideals?

On the eve of the celebration of our 200th birthday, these questions should give the Bicentennial its true meaning rather than the commercialism that is already competing for center stage. The spirit of '76 has long been on sale. Businessmen have invented a wide collection of revolutionary items ranging from $1 Bicentennial ballpoint pens to $875 scale models of the Liberty Bell. There are copies of colonial spice boxes, shaving dishes and even Dolly Madison's clothespins.

There is a better way to celebrate this nation's Bicentennial. We can rededicate ourselves to the great ideals and values upon which this nation was founded. There are important social forces in motion now that speak to the essence of what our country is all about. One is regarding the effort to give the government back to the people. Another is the effort to bring about equal opportunity among all men, regardless of race, creed, religion, or sex.

Let us compare the social forces which inspired the creation of this country two hundred years ago with those of today. Then we can better decide what should be the direction and goals of this country for the years to come. Immediately, it becomes apparent that after two hundred years there is not justice nor equality for all. Many Americans still do not have the right to the pursuit of happiness. It seems to me that a rededication to these goals should be the focus of our celebration—or else we have nothing to celebrate.

Delivered on June 6, 1976
WISN Radio, Milwaukee, Wisconsin

Focus On the Values That Make America Great

During this divisive time in our nation, what would happen if we all paused to focus on the principles that make America great? What would happen if we put our political, partisan, and selfish issues aside and focus on what is best for this country? We are at a critical crossroads. The very fabric of what defines America seems to be unraveling in front of our very eyes.

Even though America is far from perfect, there have been principles that we, as citizens, have adhered to. We value individual rights. We value freedom of speech. We value representative government, where we expect those we vote for to function in the best interests of ourselves, families, communities, and yes, our country! We value patriotism and love of country.

These are just a few of the principles we honor and respect. There are many more outlined in our Bill of Rights, and the Constitution of the United States. During this very partisan and potentially destructive time in our nation's history, we need to take time to revisit and discuss these critical documents. We need to do so with our family, friends, and in community forums.

We need to focus on the principles that make America great during a time when they seem minimized or forgotten. If we fail to do so, we may find ourselves vulnerable and carried on a path that will not be good for this country nor its citizens.

Most of us value honestly and integrity from elected officials and government employees just as we do from others that we interact with as we go about our daily lives. During these impeachment hearings, and the divisive, false, impartial information that surround them, our attention to truth and values are more important than ever. Listen critically. Focus intently.

Passive, intermittent attention on what is occurring is simply not enough.

Are the principles and practices that you value still being upheld by those in leadership positions at the local, regional, and national level of our governmental system? As difficult as it might appear, we cannot afford to turn a blind disinterested eye. There is too much at stake not to focus on the principles and values that make America great. Especially now.

Not only is the quality of life as we know it at risk. How America will operate in the future is at stake. If you love America, as imperfect as it may be, promote and focus on the values and principles that make America great.

Published November 18, 2019
https://janicesellis.com/blog

Removal of Confederate Monuments

The removal of Confederate monuments will not get rid of the great racial divide that is on display all across America. Bigotry, racism, prejudices, disenfranchisement of groups of people based strictly on skin color and economic station in life will still be an ugly part of America.

The removal of Confederate monuments will not stop how Black people are perceived and treated in the workplace all over America.

The removal of Confederate monuments will not stop how Black people are treated by police and the criminal justice system; when Blacks are stopped more often than whites with or without a legitimate reason; when once they are in the justice system, they receive longer and harsher sentences and judgements than whites for the same or lesser offenses. This is commonplace in towns and cities all across America.

The removal of Confederate monuments will not stop the perpetuation of the education achievement gap where black children are still locked in poor inferior schools; where black children who are in racially integrated schools are disciplined and expelled at much higher rates than white children for the same behavior and infractions.

The removal of Confederate monuments will not rid this country of the entrenched racism, economic and educational disparities that are the real problems. The Confederate Flag, monuments of generals that fought to maintain slavery and the southern way of life, committing acts of treason in the process, are just symptomatic of the racial problem that remains in America. Removing those symbols will only be a surface fix.

The removal of Confederate monuments will not erase the ugly history of America, and more importantly, the bane of evil that still remains as seen in the resurgence and boldness of white supremacy and blatant expressions of racial hatred.

Only facing this scourge, confronting it, and actively taking the necessary steps to make things better will have lasting meaning.

Sadly, even then, there will be those who will stay stuck in the false sense of racial superiority that is merely a relic of America's past.

Yes, Confederate flags and monuments are historical relics that too many are trying to preserve not because of their place in America's history, but in an attempt to determine America's future.

Published August 27, 2017
https://janicesellis.com/blog

Confederate Statues and Memorabilia Belong in Museums

Confederate statues and memorabilia belong in museums and designated parks to remind all Americans of a period in this nation's history that was detrimental, inhumane, ugly, and which should never be repeated. It is enough to have lingering vestiges of racial conflict, inequality, and oppression prevalent today and still holding us back. There is no need to have statues to be in public places as stark reminders.

However, toppling, tearing down, and destroying statutes and monuments, of those who were so pro slavery and led the charge to secede from the Union, is not the answer either. The resulting Civil War threatened the very existence of this country. What is the purpose of waving the confederate flag instead of or alongside the American flag? That flag along with confederate statutes and memorabilia belong in museums and designated parks.

Removing those statues and monuments will not undo history. Such actions will not undo the horrible deeds of those men, nor the lasting destructive attitudes, laws, and practices that resulted from them.

But neither is displaying them, honoring them in public squares and other public spaces of southern cities, towns, and state capitals. They only serve to make a statement that this part of American history is laudable and something to be proud of. Sadly, many Americans who regale in those times and symbols will likely continue to do so in their hearts and minds. Confederate statues and memorabilia belong in museums and designated parks.

Much of American history is preserved in national and local museums where it is accessible to anyone who would like to revisit our past, visit it for the first time, or learn anew the real facts. It is long past time that America's confederate history takes it rightful place within the walls of a national museum or several museums. Those reminders need not be destroyed. Future generations need to know the complete story of America's history—the good, the bad, along with a promising future.

It is healthy to acknowledge that any period of human enslavement, oppression, servitude, and persecution in a country's history is, indeed, a shameful and inglorious one. It begs the question why would any decent, compassionate, ethical, if not God-fearing, person want to honor and revel in such a time with visible reminders. Confederate statues and memorabilia belong in museums and designated parks along with other relics of America's past.

The goal should not be to destroy history, but to learn from it. The outrage that we are witnessing in city streets and at historical sites across America is a cry for us to learn from out past, and to begin to take meaningful and lasting actions to change it.

One united America—makes the future America a special and better place for everyone.

Published June 23, 2020
https://janicesellis.com/blog

Our Sense of Self, Family, Community, and Country Begins at Home

The first holiday of summer, Memorial Day, is a great demonstration of how our sense of self, family, community, and country begins at home. At least it should. It is also a time to see, on display, our sense of respect, duty, and honor.

Now that the picnics and patriotic activities are over, we as Americans should be filled with the real meaning of why we pause to remember those who have paid the ultimate price to keep this country secure, to enable us to continue to live free. It is more than a national holiday, a tradition.

The lasting question is: what are we to do as recipients, as beneficiaries of those who paid the ultimate price on our behalf, for our well-being? What can we do to live up to, and be deserving?

We can do a lot. We can commit and give something back in exchange for this gift of life, for the freedoms we enjoy.

Where and how do we begin? The old adage, "Everything begins at home" rings true when we think about it.

It can be argued that what is happening in the community in which we live, and in communities all across America, is a direct result of the foundation we passed, or failed to pass, onto our children in the home environment— from one generation to the other, directly, or indirectly; what our children are taught, or learn by association have far-reaching impact, lasting consequences.

It is in the home that a child first develops a sense of self, whether they feel worthy or unworthy; a sense of family, whether it is a safe and loving place, or one filled with strife and dissension.

It is in the home where one gains a sense of how he/she is to treat a neighbor, a stranger; a sense of how to care for and promote the well-being of the community, the country.

But irrespective of our views about government, taxes, and the current state of politics on the local or national stage, what are we doing—each of us—to pass on a sense of the things that really count to those whom we can influence. There are people all around each of us that we are influencing whether we are aware of it, or not.

What messages are we sending, what examples are we setting when it comes to: How we should see and treat our fellowman, irrespective of the place of their birth, irrespective of their station in life, irrespective of the color of their skin, irrespective of their political or religious persuasion.

What are we teaching our children, and how are we leading by example, when it comes to our shared responsibilities for the well-being of our family, our fellowman, our community, our country? How do we transfer a sense of respect, honor, duty?

No doubt, there is more than one way to address these important areas of nurturing. But, what an awesome responsibility each of us has, and that we all share.

Published May 28,2019
https://janicesellis.com/blog

Questions We Should Ask This Memorial Day

As we visit cemeteries, place flags, hold ceremonies, and gather for family picnics, there are questions we should ask this Memorial Day—each of us as Americans. We all should be asking questions this Memorial Day as we honor those who gave their lives in order for us to continue to enjoy the rights, privileges, and opportunities that define America.

But are we? Just look around at the issues, problems, and behaviors that we are dealing with in communities all across this nation that are so un-American. If we bother to stop and think, no doubt we all could produce our own lists of areas that desperately need work.

A very obvious one: First, and foremost, is the freedom and integrity of the press. Without a free and honest press, a fundamental tenet of a democratic society is gravely at risk. Is the press in America free? Is it practicing the highest standard of integrity? These are questions we should ask this Memorial Day because many died to protect this critical freedom.

There are many who have access to the media who are hell-bent on promoting distortions, falsehoods, downright lies to influence a public who is unable to see firsthand or bear witness that something happened or was said. Yet those the public counts on, leaders and members of the press, too often are loose with the truth. Why? What purpose does in serve other than to promote some selfish agenda rather than what is in the best interest of a trusting public? These are questions we should ask this Memorial Day.

Other critical questions include: Why are there many efforts occurring to make it more difficult for legal citizens to exercise their right to vote? Isn't the right to vote fundamental to what it means to be an American? Is the right to vote one of the privileges for which the men and women we honor today died? At this stage in American history, shouldn't the priority be to make voting equally accessible for all citizens?

There are many more questions we should ask this Memorial Day.

All around us, there are things occurring daily that threaten to undo for what so many of our fellow citizens made the ultimate sacrifice. And, if we do not stand and fight to protect the rights and privileges that make America who she is, then our commemorations ring hollow. If we are not doing what we can do to preserve what many died for, then we are failing to carry on.

How do we honor those who made the ultimate sacrifice as we go about our daily lives? Do you feel that some basic rights and privileges they fought and died for are at risk? What are you prepared to do about it? These are questions we should ask this Memorial Day. But not just today.

Published May 31, 2021
https://janicesellis.com/blog

Gifts and Gadgets Takeover

Gifts and gadgets need not take over the holiday season. As we celebrate the season, let us also recommit to celebrating family and human values, particularly when it comes to our children.

Gifts and gadgets have their place. But so does guidance of a child in helping him or her determine what is enormously important in this life. Too often, we as adults enter the world of a child where toys and things are paramount in their minds, and we indulge them rather that allow those toys and things to be a teaching opportunity.

If we are to prepare those young impressionable minds to be good sisters, good brothers, good cousins, good friends, and ultimately good parents, good neighbors, good productive citizens, then we need to seize every available teachable moment to impart something of value. Something that will help shape them, and guide them as they face life's circumstances, challenging and opportunities.

Spending quality time with our children should be an everyday thing. But sometime the holiday season offer a myriad of opportunities to drive a few important lessons home. Lessons like giving of one's time, talent, and resources to those less fortunate. Lessons like sharing some of your most prized possessions – Ninja Turtle, Dora the Explorer, X-Box, Wii, whatever the indulgent craze – with others.

Selfishness is natural. A generous and giving heart is learned. Lessons like teaching the value of no, and delayed gratification. Just because you want it today does not mean you get it today. That simply is not the way life is.

My, my, what teachable moments. Let us not miss them. There really is nothing cute about being selfish and mean or not thoughtful toward others or throwing temper tantrums because one could not have his/her way. And let us not underestimate a child's ability to understand. Can they work a video game, the computer?

We have only to look around us to realize that we need to pay attention—quality attention—to our children. We are still plagued by the phenomenon of kids resorting to killing anyone in their view at school to address what frustration that ails them.

These incidents happened in the most unsuspecting places. What does that tell us? School shootings occur almost monthly. We have been reminded much too often that we are missing the mark somewhere.

In reality, the shooting incidences are the exceptions. There are many kids crying out for attention and direction who do not resort to such extremes. As adults, we just need to be mindful. Not get caught up in our own priorities and overlook the needs of the young impressionable minds right under our noses.

Shoving toys their way or putting them in front of a television or whatever we do to avoid spending quality time will ultimately take its toll. A price will be paid.

We can do without the horrific wake-up calls of gun violence in schools, runaways, teen parents, drug, and alcohol abuse, and all the other detrimental options for our children to choose because they feel unloved or unwanted.

Let us not lose the real meaning of the holiday season. A time to gather family and loved ones together to really show care and concern about what is happening in their lives. Take advantage of those teachable and caring moments.

Find them throughout the year. Making a lasting difference in a life is what really matters.

We need to pay attention to the gifts and gadget takeover. Gifts and gadgets will come and go. But guidance and lessons for life can last forever.

Published December 22, 2014
https://janicesellis.com/blog

Holiday Season Begs Broader Conversations

Thanksgiving—a time to give thanks, but also an opportunity to try to help our families and neighbors gain a perspective on what must seem like a perpetual sea of un-welcomed changes.

Where has our once relatively tranquil and somewhat predictable American way of life gone? How has and how will the war with Iraq and possibly Afghanistan change our lives? Will there be more terrorist attacks in or near our own backyards? In the coming months, will the economy continue to get better or worse?

As we pause to find some measure of comfort in old family traditions, get reacquainted with family and friends, and take time to prepare old homemade meals almost in defiance of the instant carefree and microwave era, we will unlikely be able to escape the anxiety we feel, the loss of a sense of collective safety and control we once took for granted.

Our anxiety is greater because the global civilized world we thought was emerging only a few years ago, making us one large community, now seems rifted with cultural, religious, and economic chasms so wide that they appear to be permanent divides. What a difference of historic proportions a year, a month a day can make.

But is it really some truncated period of time, or a few cataclysmic incidents that have brought such anxiety about? The state affairs—both in this country and abroad—did not come about in a short period of time or with a few horrific incidents. That infamous day, 9/11, the terrorist alert system, the subsequent wars, the near collapse of our financial industry just got more of our attention.

The forces, evil and otherwise, that brought us to this point in human civilization have been brewing for a long, long time. And unfortunately, many of us still may not have gotten the messages.

Some of us not only still long for the way things used to be, but we also actually believe that things have not changed. Too many of us expect to go on with our lives, our dreams, and our celebrations just as we always have in the sovereign American way, ignoring all the winds of change around us.

Since change is inevitable—good or bad—why not make it work for the best? Could it be that amid all the pain, uncertainty, and compromised sense of safety that we all feel, there is greater opportunity to reconnect with some fundamental and inescapable tenets of a healthy society that we may have lost sight of?

What meaningful reflections could inform our discussion around our Thanksgiving dinner tables? What is our role in fostering positive societal outcomes? Might there be value in having a conversation with our children, our future leaders, which impresses upon them a few valuable lessons:

- As much as they have been told or would like to believe, they are not the center of things. No individual, race, or country is the center of the universe. We all occupy space. We all have purpose and roles to play.
- The quality of one's life need not be built on the backs of other human beings. The oppressed eventually rises. History is replete with examples.
- One does not have to go about his or her daily affairs with utter, even partial, disregard for their neighbor, colleague, friend, relative or stranger.
- Ignorance, perhaps, is bliss, only in love and only for a time. Ignorance generally is the breeding ground for vulnerability, keeping one who remains so at a disadvantage.
- Burying one's head in the sand solves nothing. We learned that from the ostrich.

As we begin our celebration of this holiday season, perhaps it should be more than tradition as usual. Tradition as usual may have allowed us to become complacent and accepting of the religious fanaticism right here on American soil and abroad. The wanton and rampant greed that bestow untold riches at the expense of the unsuspecting. We have either not paid very much attention, or we have been totally oblivious to many ugly forces that reign in our immediate and distant world.

Religious intolerance and racial hatred are not new. Unfortunately, they occupy too many pages in the history of too many countries. They are the ties of human nature that bind us—the ugly equalizer. How much longer can we afford to refuse to see, acknowledge and try to understand the different among us, rather than shun, alienate, or exploit them?

The many things we take for granted have often made it easy for us to ignore an age-old premise: It is the kinship, and mutual respect afforded to and by each of us around the table of humanity which will ultimately save us, or the lack thereof that will ultimately bring our own demise. This holiday season let us begin to advance the conversation.

Published November 25, 2002
The Kansas City Star

Rejuvenation of the Will, Real Gift of the Season

Perhaps one of the greatest gifts of the holiday season is the opportunity to reflect and become rejuvenated, re-energized about the true meaning of life, family, and friends.

For a moment, we can put politics aside. We can escape the piles on our desks, the backlog on the assembly line. For a moment, maybe our troubles will be out of mind and out of site long enough to allow us time to revisit what we should be about at whatever stage of life we find ourselves.

We can begin with the obvious. Irrespective of our ethnic group, religious affiliation, or location on the planet, this is the season where we pause to celebrate a major event of spiritual significance in our collective lives. We pay respect, homage, and honor to someone greater than we, who gave and sacrificed much more than we ever would dream of, and whose life and legend we still seek to understand and embrace.

Irrespective of our religious beliefs, we search to understand and practice the ageless precepts and principles in which we fervently believe. We return repeatedly to those teachings for better understanding. We urge our family and friends to get to know the one greater than we, and we encourage them to learn more about the teachings on how to live a meaningful life—for oneself and toward one's fellowman.

But let us not stop there. Amid all the festivities, my wish is that each of us make sure that we stop and find a serene and special place, take the time, to revisit and reflect on the meaning of this temporal life and our individual purpose in it.

Let this be our special gift to ourselves to become renewed in our purpose and resolve.

That irrespective of our plight in life—and each one of us carry our own set of burdens—we find the resolve to recommit ourselves to putting into practice the great gifts and guidelines for life that were passed to us by those gone before and whom we celebrate.

The presents we exchange, the meals and festivities we share are mere symbols of what we should be about every day. Albeit, and not necessarily on such a grand frenetic and frantic scale. But every day, we should be giving—giving of our time and resources to others to make a difference in their lives, starting with family and spreading abroad. We should, on a daily basis, break bread and celebrate some aspect of life with someone.

These are the real and lasting gifts of the season. If we practice, all year through, just some of the goodwill of the season, just some of the generosity of spirit, just some of the lavishness of gift giving, perhaps we could see some powerful things happening around. Maybe we could have the meaning and impact of Christmas, Hanukkah, Kwanza, or whatever your commemorative event, every day.

Perhaps, we could put a smile on a child's face, a new purpose in a teenager's life, a ray of hope for someone who is down and out and do not see his or her way. Perhaps we could put a big dent in hungry and homelessness, drug and substance abuse, gun violence, suicide and school violence, broken families, and broken homes.

Maybe, amid all the gaiety and the glitter of the season, if we continue to celebrate the true meaning of the season long after the lights are turned off, long after decorations have been dismantled, long after the ornaments and rituals have been put away—then maybe all the fuss and expense will have been worth it.

What are you really celebrating this season, and why?

How can you make the celebration even more meaningful in your everyday life? And will what you remember and take away from this season's celebration make you look forward to next season with even greater anticipation?

Amid all the hustle and bustle of the season, we will do well to find a quiet place and ponder its true meaning.

Happy rejuvenation.

Published December 26, 2000
The Kansas City Star

Messages Our Celebrations Send

What we celebrate defines what is important to us. This is abundantly clear when we think of our holidays, and what we celebrate as organizations, as families.

But what we honor and celebrate leave indelible impressions, particularly on our youth. And, perhaps, we need to be more mindful of that not just on big holidays, but every day.

So often, we as a society, speak out of both sides of our mouths. Or we too often contradict our words with our actions. Just take a look at how we celebrate athletic achievement versus academic excellence. Which gets the most fanfare? The most attention and notoriety?

The answer is pretty obvious. We have only to think of the coverage of a sports event versus the national spelling bee.

But what messages are we sending our children when we stop short of turning cartwheels in the stands and losing our voice when we watch an exceptionally skilled athlete in a sporting event? How do we celebrate exceptional academic or technical achievement? Where is the fanfare? And at what level do we bother to celebrate?

These are questions that need to be seriously considered at the family, institutional and community level—if not indeed the national level. We all know the names Michael Jordan, Larry Bird, Tiger Woods, Pete Sampras, Venus Williams, and Mia Hamm. There is no doubt, countless others would come to mind if we spent a few minutes in conversations about sports with any young person—and not so young for that matter.

But can they name a young geneticist who has made a significant advance in finding a cure for cancer or a vaccine to cure AIDS? Or a young person who spends countless hours volunteering to help the elderly, the homeless, or being a big sister or brother for a girl or boy at risk?

While these great contributions may not be things that celebrity and glamour and instant fame are made of in our society, it does not mean they should not be. These humanitarian giants certainly are not the people sought after for TV, radio, and newspaper ads. And you certainly will not find them on a box of Cheerios. But why not? We might be very surprised about the positive impact.

Yes, I know. Advertisers are interested in sales and the money that will result. But if we are not careful, too much emphasis on money and commercialism will be self-defeating in our efforts to instill the right values in our young people. Glorifying athletic achievements at the sacrifice or diminution of other accomplishments will continue to send our children mixed messages or cause other negative effects.

Remember the Columbine High School shootings? While this is an example of the extreme—that thank goodness—in the aftermath, both parents and school officials acknowledged that the status of the "jocks" at the schools (rightly or wrongly) had some role in that dreadful event. I am sure we all have school day memories of who was glorified on campus vs. who was not.

We, as parents, as communities, need to re-examine what we praise, what we celebrate, at what decibel, and why? More importantly, we need to make sure that there is enough to go around for all of the wonderful accomplishments that occur in so many areas that are important to the quality of life, the health of our society.

We need to make sure our young people feel just as good about being accomplished scholars, civic leaders as athletes.

Many parents, schools, coaches, knowingly or unknowingly encourage, indeed push, youngsters every day to be the star player in basketball, soccer, baseball, track, tennis—whichever sport of choice. And too often this is done, if not at the sacrifice of achieving academic excellence, at the significant compromise of educational achievement. And certainly, the praise and celebration are rarely comparable.

For the sake of all of our young people who are accomplishing noble and worthy feats every day, let us spread the celebration, the recognition around.

As parents, as institutions, as a city, and as a society, let us put our emphasis and appreciation in more of the right places.

Especially for our young people.

Published May 30, 2000
The Kansas City Star

Holiday Seasons Lasting Meaning

This holiday season let us find some lasting meaning that will carry us to new heights of understanding, appreciation as we relate to our loved ones, our neighbors, and the larger community of which we are a part.

Traditionally, the season begins with and culminates with the celebration of the dawn of a New Year. It is a time for shopping, feasting, partying, and much merriment. For some, it is the most joyous time of the year, with all the decorations and holiday signs and one happy event after the other.

But, for some, it is the beginning of a stressful time, even depressive time, for any number of reasons. While many of us may be fortunate to be able to enjoy the holiday season and its trappings with family and friends, there are those who see little to celebrate and have even less with which to celebrate. For them, the holiday season is only the beginning of a dreaded time—a season filled with reminders of families that were, wish lists that remain unfilled, and dreams that always seem beyond one's reach.

Too often, much of this "state of want" or "painful emptiness" has nothing to do with money or other material things. Rather, it has all to do with how one views life and his or her purpose in it. We too often let our well-being be determined by unimportant and fleeting things. Consequently, our sense of self-worth and the value we bring to those around us and the community of which we are a part get lost and we suffer immeasurably—in ways that are not always obvious.

If we take time to reflect on our world both near and afar, we all see the signs of the toll life styles and misplaced emphasis have taken on the human spirit. This year alone, we have witnessed plenty, unprecedented acts of violence by young and old alike, by the materially well off and the not-so-well off, by the sane and the not so sane. Unspeakable acts of violence in often what we thought were the most secure and sacred of places.

If we bothered to reflect on the state of the human condition in our supposedly advanced society during the past decade or two, we would have even more to be concerned about when we really look at the entire picture.

When we discover how little progress we truly have made in some of the most important areas that count, it should give us pause whether it is in the area of race relations, parenting, building healthy family units, eradicating hunger, the war on terror here in the United States and abroad, eliminating homelessness, reducing drug and substance abuse. The list goes on.

While we, as a nation, as a city, as a community, or as a family unit, undoubtedly have a lot to celebrate, we need to keep in mind how far we have yet to go in a number of areas to advance the overall well-being of humankind. Whether it is in our home, our neighborhood, our schools, or some other corner of our immediate or global community, all the scientific, technological, and medical advances will not fix a down-trodden human spirit.

Perhaps this holiday season could serve as a source of rejuvenation, recommitment to make things better for others—people and conditions we encounter every day.

Published December 22, 2014
https://janicesellis.com/blog

Thanksgiving Means More Than Tradition

Thanksgiving means more than tradition and a national holiday. It means more than cooking a great family meal, filled with foods from our favorite recipes that have been passed down from generation to generation, along with a few new salads or desserts mixed in.

Thanksgiving is a holiday uniquely American that was originally designed for the early pilgrims that settled these shores to pause and give thanks by sharing the bounty of their harvest with families and the Native Americans who had been such helpful neighbors.

The original meaning of the holiday was certainly honorable and laudable. But the sharing of the feast proved not to be enough, within itself, to foster an ongoing healthy relationship between the early settlers and the natives who were here before them. Some of the unflattering chapters in American history and the Indian reservations that are almost hidden from view are stark reminders.

What has happened to the Native Americans who first welcomed and assisted the pilgrims and early immigrants is an example of the ugly side of human nature on a large, societal, and global scale. But what is the state of relations with family members, neighbors, friends, colleagues, and others who once welcomed, embraced, shared, and helped you along? Is it as good as it ever has been, even better? Or has it slipped into a negative and toxic state, which is barely bearable if you are unsuccessful in totally avoiding it?

We have all heard family stories of Thanksgiving dinners and gathering degenerating into an unpleasant experience, if not total mayhem, because of the presence of an undesirable uncle, aunt, or sibling, or because some thoughtless full of vibrato show-off insists on uttering an insensitive and insulting comment.

Yes, it is true. Unlike friends, we cannot select our family members, and in many instances even our neighbors or colleagues. But we can most decidedly choose what Thanksgiving means to us. Making the proverbial trek to the family gathering place, overeating to the point of discomfort, and tolerating the undesirables in attendance, aside.

Thanksgiving means more than tradition. It can start with being thankful for all the countless and incredible facets of this magnificent world creation, this intelligent design of an awesome God that is there for us to experience some aspect of it every day. We can choose to be thankful and learn from the good and bad elements of the people, places, and things that we encounter along the way, on any given day in our lives. For there is purpose and meaning to be gained from it all.

So, what are you thankful for not just this Thanksgiving, for it is simply a national reminder, but every day? How do you speak your thankfulness? How do you live it? How to you show it? How do you share it?

Thanksgiving means more than tradition for this nation, and for each of us.

Published November 24, 2015
https://janicesellis.com/blog

Tough Times Can Make the Thanksgiving Holiday All the More Special

This year with the state of our national economy—many Americans having lost their jobs, homes, businesses, even hope—the meaning of Thanksgiving is all the more special.

As we gather with family and friends, perhaps with a less-bountiful table, it is still a wonderful time to find some lasting meaning that will carry us to new heights of understanding, appreciation as we relate to our loved ones, our neighbors, and the larger community in which we are a part.

Staying positive and hopeful is so important, especially during these trying times for our families and our nation.

As tough as it is on the economic and political fronts, it still can be a time for celebration but also a time to stop, reflect and regain resolve to keep moving forward in whatever way we can irrespective of the conditions in which we find ourselves. It is definitely the time to keep in our individual and collective conscience the age-old adage, "Hope reigns eternal."

While we are hopeful, we must reach out to others to help them regain or remain hopeful. During these tough times, we cannot minimize that for some, it is the beginning of a stressful time, even depressive time for any number of reasons. This has been true during the best of economic times.

While many of us may be fortunate enough to be able to enjoy Thanksgiving and all of its trappings with family and friends, there are those who see little to celebrate and have even less with which to celebrate. For them, Thanksgiving is only the beginning of a dreaded time—a season filled with reminders of families that were, wish lists that remain unfilled, and dreams that always seem beyond one's reach.

How good it would be if we could just remember and impart that, too often, much of this "state of want" or "painful emptiness" has nothing to do with money or other material things. But instead, it has all to do with how one views life and his or her purpose in it. Too often, we let our well-being be determined by unimportant and fleeting things. Consequently, our sense of self-worth and the value we bring to those around us and the community in which we are a part get lost and we suffer immeasurably—in ways that are not always obvious.

Often, one of the best ways to improve our personal condition is to look beyond it to the condition of someone else whether it is in our home, our neighborhood, our schools, or some other corner of our immediate or global community.

As bad as it may seem, it can always be worse. Make this a very special Thanksgiving with meaning, meaning that will last this entire Holiday Season and beyond.

Published November 18, 2011
USAonRace.com

Let This Thanksgiving Holiday Be Filled with Ethnic and Cultural Inclusiveness

As we join our family and friends to celebrate a holiday that is uniquely American, let us take time to reflect on the true meaning and history of Thanksgiving.

The first Thanksgiving holiday occurred during our colonial days where the newly arrived settlers along with the native American Indians came together to celebrate and share the fruit of the harvest. Irrespective of the color of their skin, their heritage, history, cultural, or ethnic uniqueness, they were grateful and thankful that they had planted and yielded great crops during, what was certain to be, difficult times in the early days of the founding of this country.

Native America Indians and the newly arrived immigrants shared in and celebrated a common humanity.

Through the centuries and across generations that make up the ethnic, racial, and cultural diversity that is quintessential America, we continue to celebrate Thanksgiving. But has its meaning changed?

How much do we reach out to include people of different racial and ethnic origins in our Thanksgiving meals, celebrations, festivities? Has our own personal table narrowed or expanded when it comes to openly including and embracing the foods, traditions, and uniqueness from the celebration of others?

What a great opportunity to learn, to explore, to embrace and expand our understanding of people and traditions differ than our own. Who will you be bringing home for dinner? Or, where will you venture out to meet and share a meal unlike you have shared in the past or add something new to spice up a family tradition?

Growth requires us stepping out beyond our comfort zones, taking chances to understand, and be understood.

The early Pilgrims and the Native American did. And for a great time, they all were the better for it.

We can reclaim their spirit and make it even greater and more inclusive today, sharing the traditions of others in person or in conversation.

Have a great Thanksgiving Holiday!

Published November 11, 2011
https://janicesellis.com/blog

Native American Nicknames and Mascots Pile Insult on Top of Injury

How long will it take us to admit and correct the injury and insult that is piled on by the continued use of Native American Nicknames and Mascots by high school, college and professional sports?

Haven't we as a nation done enough to Native Americans?

First, we came to this country pilfered and pillaged their villages, women and children. We ultimately took the land and herded them off to reservations. They continue to be subjected to sub-standard education and poor health care.

As if this wanton and utterly disenfranchisement was not enough, we have continued to reduce their culture for our entertainment by using Native American nicknames and mascots – from the genre of western film (The Lone Ranger and beyond) to our national pastime of sports, baseball and football most notably. Worse, we pass this on to our children.

Recently, the cry of "enough" has grown louder. The Smithsonian Museum of Native American History recently held a day-long symposium about whether the pro football team, the Washington Redskins, should consider changing their name and mascots. The mayor of Washington, D.C., sensitive to the issue has begun to use the "Washington Football Team" instead of the Washington Redskins.

During that day-long symposium, many attendants became sensitized to what Native Americans must feel when they see fans dressed as Indians and performing moves and dances that they haven't a clue of their sacred meaning.

There were many converts during that symposium, many vowing never to wear war paint, don an Indian feathered headdress and mockingly perform an Indian dance, "the Tomahawk Chop," again. Such use of Native American nicknames and mascots show racial and ethnic insensitivity and ignorance of history.

A few months ago, the Michigan Department of Civil Rights filed a complaint with the U.S. Department of Education, requesting that all Michigan high schools be barred from using Indian nicknames and imagery as their school mascots.

An editorial appearing in a Michigan paper, The Holland Sentinel, says it well: "...White Americans who blithely adopt for their own entertainment images from a minority group, especially one as persecuted through history as Native Americans, are likely to offend that group. The portrayals are almost inevitably one-dimensional caricatures, perpetuating old stereotypes. Too many people who would never dream of wearing blackface or a serape and sombrero abandon their good judgment when it comes to Native Americans, reducing an entire culture to war paint and feathered headdresses. If you wouldn't flaunt these images on a reservation, then they're not appropriate in a Michigan high school either."

The controversy of the use of "Redskins" by the Washington, D. C. professional football team continues to be in the news and has come full circle. It seems the use of the "Redskins" will prevail—at least for now.

As a nation, a day-long symposium or a filed complaint, and other actions here and there are starts to take corrective actions. But, they clearly are not enough. The pervasive, persistent and insensitive use of Native American Nicknames and Mascots in our most endeared sports at every level only reinforces the need for a public dialogue in communities across America.

Not to have these honest dialogues is to continue to perpetuate our attitudes toward race and ethnicity in this country, which we all can acknowledge are still in need of major, major, major adjustments.

Published November 27, 2013
https://janicesellis.com/blog

Juneteenth Celebrates Only the End of One Form of Slavery

For black Americans, Juneteenth only celebrates the end of one form of slavery—human chattel, bought and sold to the highest bidder for more than two hundred years. Blacks were forcibly brought to America in 1619 to work the soil and perform all kinds of meaningful labor, without pay, to help build America.

From 1619 to 1863, it was legal, part of a proud culture to breed Black people to be sold at auctions to the highest bidder. It was a common, accepted, and expected practice to separate families, robbing children of their biological fathers and mothers. Lashing bare backs of black men for the least of reasons ruled the day.

Hunting black men down like wild game, with dogs and guns, was the sport of choice, whether the black man had managed to escape or was deliberate let loose for the chase. Raping, taking sexual advantage of subservient helpless black women at will, siring children, whenever the desire hit the master of the plantation were common occurrences.

These kinds of practices became illegal with the passing of the Emancipation Proclamation in 1863, at the end of the Civil War, which Juneteenth commemorates. The first celebration did not occur until 1865. That speaks volumes within itself. But Juneteenth only celebrates the end of one form of slavery, the most obvious, brutal, dehumanizing kind.

Look at the kind of slavery that took the place of the horrendous legal institution. After black men were supposedly set free, for decades and even occasionally today, they were hunted down by hooded men riding horses in their ghostly robes and hanged with nooses from a tree. The noose is still often used today as a reminder.

Chasing black men down, shooting them in the back, placing a knee on the neck, using a choke hold under the guise of good policing and law and order have taken the place of the chase in the woods and the hanging from trees. So, we need to put the Juneteenth holiday in perspective. Juneteenth only celebrates the end of one form of slavery.

More broadly, since the official end of slavery, Black people (men, women, boys, and girls) for generation after generation have endured unspeakable oppression in every aspect of American life. The Emancipation Proclamation did not free Black people from rampant blatant discrimination when it comes to equal access to a quality education, decent housing, equal employment opportunities, and equal justice under the laws of the land—from voting rights to judicial rights.

Juneteenth celebrates the end of slavery. Since 1863, there has only been one oppressive degrading legal institution substituted with another insidious, often camouflaged, one that exists all across America. Juneteenth only celebrates the end of one form of slavery.

When will the current form, in all of its oppressive manifestations, end?

Published June 20, 2020
https://janicesellis.com/blog

Juneteenth Holiday but Not Voting Rights

The United States Congress manages to gain a unanimous nonpartisan vote for a federal Juneteenth Holiday, but not for voting rights. They cannot seem to agree upon a voting rights bill that would ensure that all legal citizens are able to vote. Black citizens have endured being disenfranchised and denied equal access in most aspects of American life, including the right to vote. It has been a never-ending challenge that rages on today.

Is establishing Juneteenth as a national federal holiday just a hollow symbolic gesture? Black people have declared this a national holiday in cities across America for decades to celebrate the end of slavery. So, for many Black people, declaring Juneteenth a federal holiday has little or no meaning, when many of the same elected officially are working overtime to make exercising the right to vote very difficult for Blacks. So, what does it really mean to vote for a federal Juneteenth Holiday but not for voting rights?

It would be good if designating and setting aside a day to commemorate the end of a dreadful period in American history means that all Americans will use it to work for a better coexistence. It would be good if, finally, efforts to learn about all of American history—good and bad—would be embraced and taught in schools from grade school to college. But that is not the case. Some of the same elected officials who voted for a federal Juneteenth Holiday but not for voting rights are also fighting against including the history of Blacks and the black experience in school curricula.

So, what gives? As much as one would like to believe that passage of this unanimous legislation bodes for more nonpartisan support to resolve other issues important to the citizens who put them in office, it is unlikely to be the case. Will the country be able to celebrate passage of a sensible bipartisan voting rights bill, a much-needed infrastructure bill, a good education bill that would support universal pre-K and affordable college tuition? Passage of such bills would be very meaningful for all Americans.

Black people could benefit much more if there was bipartisan support for passage of legislation in these areas. It could mean getting a better education and more access to jobs. Passage of the federal legislation for Juneteenth Holiday but not for voting rights protection, educational reform, and measures to address infrastructure issues that will improve the safety and security in many aspects of our daily lives leaves much more work to be done.

Maybe, we can continue to have hope that this Congress will pass more bipartisan legislation in areas that will make real differences in the lives of Black Americans and all Americans.

Published June 20, 2021
https://janicesellis.com/blog

Independence Day Is Not Just About Fireworks, Picnics, and Parades

As we prepare to commemorate the Fourth of July, we might do well to revisit the principles and privileges outlined in the Declaration of Independence and examine their fullest meaning in our daily lives. Not to do so is to fail to take advantage of the opportunities that come with being an American, a Kansas Citian.

As hokey as it might sound to some, it may well be worth it to pause a moment and ask, what does the Fourth of July celebration mean to me? You might even ask, what does it mean in my city, my community?

The Fourth of July celebration should be a time for each of us to take inventory of the political direction of our country, our city, our community. Are we making progress ideologically or have we abandoned our ideals? Are all citizens afforded dignity, respect, equal access, equal treatment under all the laws of the land?

The real test is: Can we see the Declaration of Independence in action, right here in Kansas City, for all Kansas Citians?

As we pause from work and gather with family and friends, perhaps discussing these questions could stimulate and inspire us to revisit the true meaning of the Constitution, the Bill of Rights and all the amendments in between. Let meaningful dialogue punctuate—it does not need to replace, but rather just be a part of—the commercialism that usually competes for center stage. Fireworks, T-shirts, and other memorabilia have their place.

Amid all the pomp, picnics, and fanfare, ponder for a moment what it means to be an American, an African American, a Hispanic American, an Asian American— whatever your racial and ethnic origin. You might examine whether you, as an individual, are truly *giving* and *living, ensuring,* and *enjoying, providing,* and *partaking* of all the opportunities this creed affords? Have you bothered to read and revisit its meaning, lately?

What is our role in ensuring that the Declaration of Independence lives?

Could it be that too often we fail to exercise one of the greatest, most powerful rights we as Americans have— speaking up and speaking out? Speaking out still gets results. America, Kansas City or needed changes in your community did not come about through silence. Nor did needed changes occur as a result of complacency, apathy, or complaining without action. Whatever gains have been made at the national, state, or local level have often been because of many people being *willing* and *courageous* enough to speak out, and get involved, when it counted.

Yet too many of us choose to remain silent about the things we see, the things we experience, the things we encounter. Our silence is often born out of fear of reprisal or feelings of frustration because we are not sure how or where we should make our observations known or voices heard.

Imagine where America would be—or would there be an America—had George Washington, Thomas Jefferson, John Adams, Thomas Payne, and countless others decided not to speak out against religious persecution, taxation without representation? Imagine where African Americans would be in this country had it not been for Frederick Douglas, Harriet Tubman, Sojourner Truth, W.E.B. DuBois, Thurgood Marshall, Martin Luther King, Jr., and countless others who spoke out and risked their lives to ensure that America's democratic principles and individual rights extended to all.

There is a meaningful way to celebrate the Fourth of July holiday. Pause a bit and rededicate yourself to the great ideals and values upon which this nation was founded. Hokey? All we need to do is think of all the anti-American sentiment right here on American soil, the vocal—and sometimes violent—vigilante groups and silent individuals who truly believe something is very wrong with our laws and choose to take the law into their own hands. Many, like our revolutionary forefathers felt toward England, feel that it is time to take arm and revolt against the current American way.

There are important social, economic, and political issues all around that will impact you, your children, your grandchildren, the future of this country.

Is it too much to expect, as we approach the holiday celebration of our nation's birth, to spend a little time discussing with our families, children, and neighbors the principles that got us here, and will keep us?

Published June 25, 2001
The Kansas City Star

Commit to Making America Better and Stronger

After being able to get back to our great tradition of celebrating the July 4th holiday, let us commit to making America better and stronger. If the pandemic and the virulent political divisions that we have experienced during the past 18 months do nothing more, it should remind us of what life can be like when we are unable to experience the wonderful privileges and opportunities this nation affords.

This Fourth of July weekend saw unprecedented levels of travel, some even more than the pre-pandemic years before. Americans were happy to take to the airways and travel the roads again to be with family and friends. To sit on the beach fronts, have picnics in the parks, barbecues in the backyards, and experience a cascade of fireworks near and far. Imagine what could happen if we commit to making America better and stronger with the same level of eagerness and excitement!

The Independence Day Celebration in Washington, DC, with the pageantry and patriotic songs and fireworks extravaganza, was so welcomed, so needed, so comforting, and so inspiring. It was not only a time to be reminded of why this nation was founded, but also to serve as impetus for each and every American to realize, want to protect those inalienable rights and privileges, and commit to making America better and stronger.

Embedded in the Declaration of Independence, the Constitution of the United States, the patriotic songs that bring both joy and tears are words and principles for which this nation continues to strive to achieve. America is by no means perfect. While much has been achieved toward making it a great nation, there is still much more work to be done. But it will not happen if each of us do not commit to making America better and stronger as we go about our daily lives and occupations.

We have only to look around and see the threat that America faces from within. The political divide is both bitter and deep. There seems to be more concern about personal positions and agendas than doing what is best for the country so that all its citizens have a chance of realizing its promises. Inward, self-centered thinking and actions rarely yield a greater good. If being able to celebrate this nation's birth as so many of us were able to do this weekend does nothing more, it should make us want to commit to making America stronger and better as never before.

After this great July 4th celebration, what are you willing to do?

Published July 5, 2021
https://janicesellis.com/blog

Beginning a New Year, a New Century
Building a Better School System

Be it resolved that we, Kansas Citians working together, will turn our school district around and create a system that will effectively educate our children.

If that is not one of our collective resolutions, as a city, it should be. Not to commit to such a resolve is truly missing the mark. With the start of a New Year, a new century, we can ill afford to forget or put on the back burner how the last one ended and what challenges it left us.

Now that daily or weekly media coverage about the imminent loss of accreditation due to poor student performance on standardized tests has subsided, it does not mean that the heat is off. The heat is on. It has been on—some would argue for years, even decades. The problem is: We, as a city, have not collectively felt the heat.

Amid all the problems with our school system, amid the alarming trend of churning out kids poorly prepared year after year, we have not felt the collective urgency to come together and stop the bleed. Stop the hemorrhage of throwing good money after bad, with truly little to show for it. Stop the cycle of instructional practices in the classroom where overall student achievement, as a whole, remains inadequate and in some cases, have actually deteriorated.

Yes, over the years and through all the turmoil, we have had some successes. There are some schools within the Kansas City district that have accomplished academic excellence—schools both widely recognized, others barely applauded. Perhaps, too few of us know those few bright spots and shinning stars. But we commend those achievements.

However, the focus of our attention must be on the plight of the nearly 32,000 students who are at risk—who are in schools and classrooms where continual poor performance is the norm.

Some see the explosion of charter schools as the answer. But even if they present a better alternative, there is not enough time or resources to have enough charter schools to solve this City's public education problem.

Some see our new superintendent as the panacea. Yes, we need a strong, committed visionary at the helm. But we are fooling ourselves to think that he, without an equally dedicated and prepared army of administrators and teachers, and tangible steadfast community support, can successfully overcome some formidable obstacles and turn this mammoth morass into an effectively functioning educational system.

Yes, some positive initiatives have occurred. Putting in procedures to improve accountability in the schools and classrooms, starting Saturday classes for those students most at risk for not making the grade—these are good steps. But to get where we need to be will take much, much more.

If we do not, as a city, come to this basic realization, the month of May (when we lose our accreditation) will come and go, and the succeeding two-year probationary period for us to regain accreditation will come and go, and we will see little appreciable improvement.

The real question is: Will we collectively answer the call to get involved in a positive way and turn our school district around?

How many of us really understand what the administrators and teachers are up against in the classrooms and beyond the classrooms to be effective, and to regain accreditation? How many of us could explain it to a colleague, a neighbor, or a concerned parent? How many of us as parents, as business leaders, as elected officials, as religious leaders, as capable community organizations, and as concerned citizens know how we can specifically help?

More importantly, how many of us fully understand the short and long-term costs and repercussions of the alternative?

Wouldn't finding out be the logical starting point?

Ensuring that our children will learn what they need to learn to effectively function in this New Year, the new century—there are few better resolutions deserving of our collective resolve.

What will you do other than sit around, shake your head, criticize, and complain?

Published January 11, 2000
The Kansas City Globe

Happy New School Year

A new school year should mean new resolves for our children. Are we commemorating a Happy New School Year with a new commitment to help our children become the very best that they can be?

For most of us adults, January marks the New Year, the time of new beginnings, eager anticipation, and renewed resolve to be, and to do, better than before. To improve and progress in those areas near and dear to us.

We celebrate and commemorate this opportunity for new and renewed beginnings in notable ways. Year after year, like clockwork.

It probably has never occurred to us that our children, depending on their age and eligibility to participate in the revelry, probably wonder what all the fuss is about, particularly our kindergartners, grade school, and middle school children.

But they have a "New Year" too, with all the elements of great anticipation, excitement, anxiety—their new school year.

Many kids, like adults, approach their new year with eagerness, and some with trepidation, about beginning another year of learning in new classrooms with new books and learning materials, with new friends, new teachers.

While many are too young to understand all this resolution business, most of our children have their desires and goals for the coming school year. They range from learning the alphabet to learning to read, from solving math problems to using the computer. Some, no doubt, aspire to have perfect attendance, write award-winning essays, join the debate team, participate in athletics, the school band.

But, more so than adults, they cannot achieve their goals alone.

That is where we come in. While children may not understand the full impact and tradition around resolving to do better and to achieve more at the beginning of a new year, we do.

Now, is the time, at the beginning of the school year, to get involved to make a difference in a child's life. We need to be asking our children and their schools, during the first weeks of school, what role we can play to improve and positively impact the learning experience in and outside the classroom.

What are your resolutions this New School Year for the children in your life?

Published August 24, 2015
https://janicesellis.com/blog

Black History Month Will Never Be Enough

For decades, the month of February has been set aside to draw attention to the contributions of African Americans, or Blacks. But Black History Month will never be enough time to adequately cover the contributions of Negroes, Blacks, or African Americans—names applied during the last 400 years.

Blacks have made significant contributions in all areas of American life, from A to Z, from the Arts to Zoology and all subjects in between. Despite arriving to this country as slaves, enduring centuries of oppression and discrimination, and despite ongoing efforts to minimize, marginalize, distort, hide—even deny and destroy—Blacks have played and continue to make major contributions in American history.

Black History Month will never be enough time to even put a dent in what Blacks across generations have achieved for this nation, in every area of American life.

In 2020, Black History Month at best is received with mixed emotions. On the positive side, it is good that at least there continues to be a meager effort to draw attention to the roles that some key Blacks have played. Historical lessons and exhibits are highlighted in schools. Communities host celebratory events. There may be a revisit of movies and documentaries on TV and in theatres.

On the negative side, these activities do not even scratch the surface of the voluminous records that exist. The featured lessons, exhibits, and celebrations tend to focus on the same few most famous Blacks. Only those who captured media attention because of the dramatic circumstances, often death, associated with their contributions. Those few are the focus and get the most attention.

One month of focus, which happens to be the shortest month, truly begs the question of whether it is merely a salvo, a feeble attempt to correct an egregious injustice perpetrated against an oppressed people. Black History Month will never be enough to correct that injustice.

What about the many, many black Americans who made significant contributions under less dramatic circumstances, in less sexy areas like in the sciences, medicine, mathematics, agriculture, mechanics, and a host of other areas?

What messages are we sending to the young impressionable minds of our children with such limited focus? Black history is American history. Until textbooks, daily classroom curricula and lessons include an accurate and complete accounting in every subject area, there is so much work to be done.

When the contributions of black Americans are put in their proper place in American history, there will be no need for designating one month out of the year as a quick fix. The stark reality is that Black History Month will never be enough to correct the record.

Published February 13, 2020
https://janicesellis.com/blog

Women's History Month Is Like Black History Month

Women's History Month is like Black History Month, woefully inadequate to celebrate, let alone cover, the myriad of roles women have played and continue to play, and the countless contributions they have made and continue to make.

While Women's History Month in the United States can trace its beginnings to the first International Women's Day held in March 1911, there were no significant or annual monthly celebration until 1987.

It was President Jimmy Carter who, by Proclamation in 1980, designated March 8 as National Women's History Week. Subsequent presidents followed suit. But it was not until 1987 that Congress passed a law designating March as Women's History Month.

Women's History Month is like Black History Month in that it has taken centuries for the significant contributions of women to be recognized at all. While there are those who would argue that one-month of recognition is better than no recognition at all, I would readily agree.

There are good things that result. There is heightened awareness, which is a great thing for little girls to see the many possibilities there are for their lives. The programs and commemorations serve as reminders to all—men, women, boys, and girls—of the abilities or women and the unswerving respect they deserve.

But Women's History Month is like Black History Month in that we often find the same names and faces remembered, honored, exhibited, and discussed in classrooms and community programs year after year. What about all those other women who go unrecognized?

Women, like Blacks, have made and continue to make significant contributions, generations after generations to American and world history. They continue to do so in every aspect of our daily lives, beginning with the priceless, irreplaceable role of motherhood. And it expands in every direction from there.

In 2020, there are very few areas, professions, or important roles in our society that women are not fulfilling and fulfilling them as well as men. But is it being captured in the history books and taught as part of American history as it rightfully should?

Women's History Month is like Black History Month, most importantly, in that it is stark evidence that we must continue to work for the day that there will be no need to set aside a month to recognize that women, like Blacks, are an integral and inseparable part of American history.

Our roles and contributions should be interwoven in every aspect of the American story, and should be taught, and spoken about at every opportunity.

Published March 19, 2020
https://janicesellis.com/blog

We Must Never Forget That Elected Officials Work for the People

Labor Day is set aside to celebrate and honor workers across many industries whose efforts keep America running each and every day.

Have you ever thought of elected officials as being part of the workforce that keeps America prosperous and working in the best way possible? More importantly, do elected officials perceive themselves as part of the American workforce? Or do they see themselves above the typical worker, perched on some lofty pedestal?

Just as importantly, does our fan club behavior contribute to how they perceive themselves, and encourage the liberties they take in doing, or not doing, their job?

As we pause this Labor Day to honor workers who contribute to the economic and social well-being of this nation, those same workers should never forget that they are employers themselves. Elected officials work for the people.

It was members of the American labor movement that fought to set aside a day to honor workers. Also, they organized labor unions to improve working conditions and achieve better wages for work performed. In many ways, that work continues today.

But back to the behavior and decisions of many elected officials who are employed and accountable to the people who voted them in office. What is their job performance, their contribution to the social and economic well-being of the people who elected them, and the nation?

Elected officials can be evaluated at the local, state, and national level by those who put them in office.

Whether or not they are performing the duties that are within their power and scope of responsibilities can be most readily observed by following the actions of the Representatives and the Senators that make up the United States Congress.

What do you think about that august body receiving an annual cost of living increase, and yet they are not able to agree upon increasing the minimum wage for the lowest paid workers in the labor force?

Many Americans are struggling to make ends meet because of low wages that are inadequate to meet the cost of living.

How many elected officials, based on their salary and access to other economic opportunities, leave office wealthier than when they arrived?

Former President Harry Truman, from the Show Me State, wrote in his diary in 1954, "An honest public servant can't become rich in politics." By implication, he is saying honest politicians should be working on behalf of the people, not themselves.

What do you think about members of Congress having access to the best health insurance policy, and yet cannot find it within themselves to create a path for every American to have access to good health care services?

Many working Americans do not have and cannot get basic health insurance for themselves or their families.

Then there is the perennial fight over the issue of fair taxation—everyone paying their fair share of taxes. Is Congress passing legislation to make sure that the people who hired them are not carrying more of the tax burden than they should?

But it is not just some members of Congress who are not performing their jobs in the interests of the people who hired them. There are state elected officials from governors to members of the legislature, mayors, county executives and their legislative bodies who are not passing laws and policies to benefit the people.

There is no greater current example of the impact of poor job performance of elected officials at all levels than how they have failed to do what is needed to help control the catastrophic effect of COVID on every aspect of American life.

At the end of the day, voters expect elected officials at all levels to work on their behalf. Policies and laws ultimately impact not only wages AND access to health care but the very quality of life from the family unit to the community, city, state, and nation.

This brings up the other side of the employer/employee relationship. For those of us who have worked in any industry, has your employer hired you and left you to your own devices, to do what you wanted without reviews or accountability? Doubtful.

We, the people, must do our jobs by holding elected officials, our employees, accountable. Elected officials should not be allowed to put their personal interests and agendas ahead of those who hired them. Other workers would never be able to get away with doing that.

Do we as a disengaged and, oftentimes, doting public assign elected officials star quality, hands-off status?

By what measures do you evaluate your elected officials? Job performance should be evaluated at every level of government. It would be best to monitor those actions along the way.

Each of us needs to ask ourselves, what kind of boss am I?

When it comes time for an office holder to be rehired, when they campaign for your vote to continue in that job, each voter has an opportunity to fire or rehire.

In the private sector, it is rare that an employee can continually hold a position when their job performance is hurting or not advancing the well-being of the company that hired them. It is no different for employees that we hire to ensure that the government functions at its very best.

Do you consider elected officials as part of the labor force being honored on Labor Day?

After all, they have one of the most important and significant jobs — working on behalf of the people, and the prosperity of America.

We must never forget that.

Published September 6, 2021
The Missouri Independent

Today, Can You Identify National Values That Unite Us As Americans?

Just two weeks ago, we paused to remember those who lost their lives on that tragic day, September 11, 2001 as the unthinkable happened: America was attacked by a foreign enemy on its own soil. In the aftermath, amid the horrid loss of life, the pierced veil of safety once thought impenetrable, the fear, and uncertainly about what was ahead, Americans seemingly became one.

Back then, in spoken and unspoken ways, the values that we held dear as Americans took over in a way that was palpable. We wore our unity on our sleeves. We rallied around those values that unite us—patriotism, our democratic institutions, freedom, protection of our collective well-being.

Fast forward to today, twenty years later, where has that sense of unity gone?

What seminal events have brought out the worse in our behavior where we often choose, unabashedly, baseness over valiance? When did it start?

The years immediately following 9/11, we were united in spirit and actions to fight against the threat of terrorism to preserve our way of life. But while we were preventing foreign terrorists from attacking us, home grown terrorists were organizing in our midst.

Our politics was not filled with virulent rancor as we have today. Compromise was still possible between the two political parties. Peddling lies and declaring fake news as real news had not become a central part of the public discourse.

Little did we know that so many Americans would accept and fall victim to the lies that have rolled and continued to roll off the lips of leaders, and that the use of fake distorted news from many media outlets and voices would become commonplace.

Also, wedged between the unity that occurred after 9/11 and the crippling divisiveness of today was the election of America's first black president.

On the surface that was a ray of hope. Many saw the election of President Barack Obama as America moving into a post-racial era.

Oh boy, were we wrong! Since the election of Obama, race relations have deteriorated and many Americans believe that the gains made over decades have been lost.

Even though Obama was elected for a second term, partisan politics in Congress worsened, with Republicans openly expressing that their goal was to defeat whatever Obama proposed. Most times, they succeeded.

Meanwhile, all across America, more disunity was brewing and gaining a foothold fueled by lies and conspiracy theories.

Pervasive among the festering dissension is the pernicious conflict and discord along racial lines, with birthers putting a national face on the issue by claiming Obama was not born here, in an attempt to make his black presidency illegitimate.

The election of Donald J. Trump as president became the catalyst and embodiment of the other America—the silent America with many grievances, primarily along racial and economic lines. During the Trump presidency the manifestations of "Them vs. Us" became manifold whether grounded in truth and facts or not.

For example, the unfounded peddling of the belief that immigrants were responsible disproportionately for rapes and the increase in crimes occurring in the United States became a mantra of which the vestiges have stuck in the minds of many.

Legislative measures to ensure equity and equal access—affirmative actions, gender equality, voting rights—became increasingly sources of contention and disagreement.

This spreading cancer of discord has metastasized into other areas such as how patriotism is defined. Brandishing white supremacy, disrespecting the flag, undermining, and attacking the foundation and institutions of our democratic form of government are increasing becoming the norm.

Another perennial divide is the continuing debate about what constitutes good gun control measures vs. Second Amendment rights. It has increased gun ownership among citizens and criminals alike that is unmatched by any other civilized nation in the world, resulting in higher rates of gun violence and gun deaths than any other civilized country.

Currently, we are living one of the greatest disagreements everyday: How do we come together to stop the catastrophic costs of the Covid pandemic.

Americans seem to be at odds about nearly everything.

Where have the values gone that once united us? Those that gave us a common sense of purpose despite those social, economic, and political areas that still need improvement?

We seem to have forgotten that unity in purpose can be achieved amid differences and imperfections. It occurs in many aspects of our daily lives.

Some would argue that the disunity that is so visible today has always been there, existing just beyond a façade of one America. That the United States of America has never been a country of states that shared binding values and principles, perhaps except when we were at war, and not always then.

Today, more and more, it seems we have only been united superficially, symbolically. Deep down, one must ask does the majority of Americans believe in values that foster a common humanity afforded all citizens regardless of race, religion, economic status, gender, or age.

Who and what America stands for is coming more into question at home and abroad.

More so than ever, America looks like a nation that is losing its identity and is struggling to define its core values and a path forward.

It is left up to us as Americans to uphold and live those values that will change the course of disunity that we are currently on.

But do we even know, anymore, what those values are, which most Americans could agree upon today, that will bind us together as a nation?

Published September 20, 2021
The Missouri Independent

Postscript: Onward and Upward

My journey in becoming an advocate journalist has not been a deliberate, well-planned pursuit. There have been many converging societal and personal forces impacting my life, oftentimes, all at once it seemed. They all have determined and impacted who I have become, and the choices I have made in fulfilling what I deem as my purpose, calling, and response to this gift of life.

The sum total of my experiences---personally, professionally, educationally, economically, socially, culturally—provide the authenticity, the authority, the mission, the grist, which I think are required, and upon which I have functioned as an advocate journalist throughout my career. I have functioned as an advocate journalist while simultaneously holding positions as a government and corporate executive, a small business owner, a mayoral candidate for a major American city, a non-profit executive before becoming a full-time advocate journalist.

Continuing to be an advocate journalist still calls.

Publication Sources of Commentaries

Selected articles for this book originally appeared in the following publications.

Online Publications:

JaniceSEllis.com Janice Ellis | Author | Life, Liberty, Pursuit of Happiness | Race | Gender (janicesellis.com), 2014—

The Missouri Independent, Missouri Independent, 2021—

RaceReport.com Race Report, 2012—2016

USAonRace.com Race Relations in The USA and Diversity News (usaonrace.com), 2007—2014

Newspapers:

Kansas City Star, 2000—2004

Kansas City Call, 2002—2007

Kansas City Globe, 1989—2007

Milwaukee Community Journal, 1983--1986

Milwaukee Business Journal, 1984—1986

Radio Stations:

WISN Radio, ABC Affiliate, 1974—1976

About the Author

Janice S. Ellis, MA, MA, PhD, a native daughter of Mississippi, grew up and came of age during the height of the Civil Rights Movement and the Women's Liberation Movement. Born and reared on a small cotton farm, she was influenced by two converging forces that would set the course of her life.

The first was the fear and terror felt by Blacks because of their seeking to exercise the right to vote along with other rights and privileges afforded whites. She became determined to take a stand and not accept the limits of that farm life nor the strictures of oppressive racial segregation and gender inequality. She aspired to have and achieve a different kind of life—not only for herself, but for others.

The second was her love of books, the power of words, and her exposure to renowned columnists Eric Sevareid of The CBS Evening News with Walter Cronkite and Walter Lippmann, whose column appeared for more than three decades in over 250 major newspapers across the United States and another 50 newspapers in Europe.

It was the study of Lippmann's books and commentary that inspired Dr. Ellis to complete a Master of Arts degree in Communication Arts, a second Master of Arts degree in Political Science, and a Doctor of Philosophy in Communication Arts, all from the University of Wisconsin. It was during her course of study that Dr. Ellis' unwavering belief—the belief that the wise use of words is what advances the good society—was solidified.

Dr. Ellis has been an executive throughout her career, first in government, then in a large pharmaceutical company, later as President and CEO of a marketing firm, and finally as President and CEO of a bi-state non-profit child advocacy agency. Along with those positions, she has been writing columns for more than four decades on race, politics, education, and other social issues for a major metropolitan daily newspaper, *Kansas City Star*; a major metropolitan business journal, *Milwaukee Business Journal*; and for community newspapers *The Milwaukee Courier, The Kansas City Globe,* and *The Kansas City Call.* She wrote radio commentary for two years for one of the largest ABC radio affiliates in Wisconsin and subsequently wrote and delivered a two-minute spot on the two largest Arbitron-rated radio stations in the Greater Kansas City area. She has also written for several national trade publications, focusing on healthcare and the pharmaceutical industry.

Dr. Ellis published an online magazine, USAonRace. com, for seven years dedicated to increasing understanding across race and ethnicity, in which she analyzed race and equality issues in America. The website continues to attract thousands of visitors per year. The site also has a vibrant

Facebook page with fans numbering in the thousands. Dr. Ellis launched a companion site, RaceReport.com, which aggregates news about race relations, racism, and discrimination from across the United States and around the world on a daily basis.

Dr. Ellis also has her own website, JaniceSEllis, which houses a collection of her writings and where she writes a regular blog. Follow her on facebook.com/janicesellis1/ and twitter.com/janicesellis1.

Her first book, *From Liberty to Magnolia: In Search of the American Dream* (2018) has received several national and international awards since its initial release. The most recent is the Independent Press Award for Race Relations (May 2020). It was noted that the competition is judged by experts from various aspects of the book industry, including publishers, writers, editors, book cover designers and professional copywriters. Selected award winners and distinguished favorites are based on overall excellence. In 2020, the Independent Press Award had entries worldwide. Participating authors and publishers reside in countries such as Australia, Brazil, Cambodia, Canada, India, Ireland, Portugal, Sweden, and others. Books submitted included writers located in cities such as Austin to Memphis to Santa Cruz; from Copenhagen to Mumbai; from Albuquerque to Staten Island; from Boise to Honolulu, and others.

Other international and national awards the book has received include: the New York City Big Book Award for

Women Issues (November 2019); the Grand Prize Journey Award for Nonfiction (April 2019) from Chanticleer International Book Reviews; the Gold Medal Award for Nonfiction Books from the Non Fiction Authors Association (May 2018), the highest award bestowed for nonfiction authors. *From Liberty to Magnolia* received a notable editorial review and honor from Kirkus Reviews, one of the oldest and most credible reviewers of books for libraries, schools, bookstores, publishers, agents, and other industry professionals. In bestowing the honor, Kirkus noted, "*From Liberty to Magnolia* was selected by our Indie Editors to be featured in *Kirkus Reviews* April 15, 2018 Issue. Congratulations! Your review has appeared as one of the 35 reviews in the Indie section of the magazine which is sent out to over 5,000 industry professionals (librarians, publishers, agents, etc.) Less than 10% of our Indie reviews are chosen for this, so it's a great honor." The book continues to receive great customer reviews on Amazon and Goodreads.

Dr. Ellis' most recent book is *Shaping Public Opinion: How Real Advocacy Journalism™ Should Be Practiced.* (2021), grand prize winner of the Nellie Bly Nonfiction Journalism Award.

www.ingramcontent.com/pod-product-compliance
Lightning Source LLC
Chambersburg PA
CBHW062121020426
42335CB00013B/1055